HEROES, VILLAINS, AND HEALING:

MARVEL EDITION

KENNETH ROGERS, JR.

HEROES, VILLAINS, AND HEALING: MARVEL EDITION

A GUIDE FOR MALE SURVIVORS OF CHILDHOOD SEXUAL ABUSE USING MARVEL COMIC SUPERHEROES AND VILLAINS

Urano
publishing

Argentina - Chile - Colombia - Spain
USA - Mexico - Peru - Uruguay

© 2024 by Kenneth Rogers, Jr.

© 2024 by Urano Publishing, an imprint of Urano World USA, Inc

8871 SW 129th Terrace Miami FL 33176 USA

Urano
publishing

Cover art and design by Luis Tinoco

Cover copyright © Urano Publishing, an imprint of Urano World USA, Inc

The first edition of this book was published in June 2024

ISBN: 978-1-953027-41-2

E-ISBN: 978-1-953027-43-6

Printed in Colombia

Library of Cataloging-in-Publication Data

Rogers, Jr., Kenneth

1. Childhood Sexual Abuse   2. Trauma & Healing

Heroes, Villains and Healing

For you, because everyone deserves to heal.

Table of contents

Part Three:
THE ROAD OF TRIALS:
Grieving, anger, and understanding it was not your fault

Part Four
TRANSFORMATION:
Breaking the silence and telling your truth

Part Five
MASTER OF TWO WORLDS:
Resolution, moving on, and post-traumatic growth

FOREWORD

Here's the reason I like Spider-Man: He did what I would've done if I had been given superpowers. At least initially. He didn't go fight crime. He didn't try to make the world better. He just wanted to make some money so he could look cool for a girl. That made sense to me. It still does. Then Spider-Man found out something that every child, teenager, and adult I've ever worked with who has experienced trauma also found out. My grandpa would phrase it this way: "You know you're a good person if your life is hard. Because the best people in the world often suffer the most. Goodness is rarely rewarded and quite often punished."

Now here is where Spider-Man went from a hero I liked to a hero I loved and respected, one who taught me far more than the adults who beat me as a child. He taught me that even though goodness is punished, even though goodness is rarely rewarded, you still do the right thing. Why? Because it's the right thing. Because with great power comes great responsibility, and true power comes from true goodness. That's when I realized Spider-Man's true superpower. His true superpower was, is, and always will be his goodness.

That's why Tony Stark wanted Spider-Man to be better than him. That's why Doctor Strange told him that he's made enough difference for a hundred lifetimes. That's why people like me not only looked up to him, but learned from him and became better men because of him. It was not the *Spider* that resonated with me and formed me into who I am today. It was the *Man* in Spider-Man that I looked up to, and I still do.

Peter led me to so many other men, women, and everything in between. To the Silver Surfer who sacrificed himself for his planet. To a family that did not start off as a family but eventually found their true power in family. To a Captain that was marvelous, and to a Hulk that was incredible. I would not have found this universe without Peter. For that, if nothing else, I will always thank him. But Peter also taught me that core lesson: To look past the *super* to what really makes a *hero*.

That's why when I met Kenneth Rogers, I knew exactly what I was looking at. I was looking at a hero. I don't think even he believed that. I very much doubt that he believes that now. That's part of what makes him a real hero. The reason I could recognize Kenny so quickly is that I had spent most of my life with Peter, Bruce, Carol, Tony, Natasha, and so many others. I recognized him so quickly because I had been taught to look past the Spider to the Man.

Kenny has the ability to help *you* not only look past the super to the hero, but also learn how to be a hero yourself. That is *his* superpower: teaching those who never thought they could be heroes how to be heroes. He learned through pain, suffering, and blood how to amplify what was within him. Many times, he feared it was darkness. But when you read his lessons, you know exactly what he amplified. He amplified the light. Kenny, like Steve Rogers, is a good man. Like Spidey, that is also his superpower.

Perhaps most importantly, Kenny does one thing I have never seen before in my entire career in the field of traumatic stress. The idea that one can use comics to help people with PTSD, depression, anxiety, etc. is not a novel idea. When applied to trauma, it can be downright dismissive sometimes, such as when people say "your trauma gave you a 'superpower.'" Kenny understands all this because *he* went through all this as a trauma survivor. No, Kenny does not oversimplify his contribution into such a naïve position. Kenny does something that I, as a clinical psychologist who has been in the field for over twenty years, have a hard time imparting not only to my patients, but to myself as a trauma survivor. I'll buy that I can "learn how to use my superpower." But until I met Kenny, I never, ever genuinely believed that I, myself, am a hero. All the national committees, all the graduate degrees, awards, and Ivy League medical school faculty appointments in the world didn't convince me that I am a hero. Kenny. Kenny did. Here's how he did it. He told me what he will tell you in this book: *You may not have been a hero yesterday, but you are today, and you will have the chance to be again tomorrow.* This is his nucleic message across all his work. All else he speaks of is focused on the mechanics, the Stark Tech, of how to accomplish this for yourself, how to look past the *super* to the *hero* inside you.

You are about to enter a marvelous universe. Kenny is the best guide I have seen in my entire career. He won't fail you. He will take you upward and onward. Excelsior.

DR. MICHAEL GOMEZ

Introduction

I have a confession to make. I'm a DC fan. I know this guide specifically discusses Marvel characters in relation to understanding and healing from the trauma of childhood sexual abuse, but in the past, Superman, Flash, and Batman were the characters I identified with most. For this reason, the first edition of this guide pertained to DC heroes and villains. For me, the DC universe seemed to make supply parallels between the challenges its heroes faced and the coping mechanisms used by survivors to get through the challenges of life created by sexual abuse.

However, after publishing the first volume of *Heroes, Villains, and Healing,* survivors, therapists, counselors, and child abuse advocates reached out to express their gratitude for having published a guide for male survivors, but they regretted that I did not include any Marvel characters. I soon realized that the same way I view my actions, thoughts, and relationships through the lens of DC heroes and villains, other survivors and the individuals who help them cope with the trauma of their past abuse, view their actions, thoughts, and relationships through the lens of Marvel heroes and villains.

Beyond a shadow of a doubt, at this moment, Marvel is more popular than DC. It's true, DC did release *Justice League*, but the Marvel universe has moved beyond comics and video games into major-grossing summer blockbusters that have a unique and often-seamless ability to meld plots of movies such as *Captain America: Civil War, Guardians of the Galaxy, Thor: Ragnorak, Spiderman: Homecoming,* and *Black Panther* into one epic tale which led to *The Avengers: Infinity Wars.* Netflix's *The Defenders,* and ABC's *Agents of S.H.I.E.L.D.* and *The Inhumans* create new lovers of the Marvel universe who would not exist if Marvel had stuck only to comic books and graphic novels. Finally, the X-Men franchise, including *Wolverine, Logan,* and the horror film *The New Mutants,* spans decades (and sometimes centuries), providing entertainment for new, old, and returning fans via reincarnations of old characters and altered origin stories. While DC's characters, movies, shows, and comics are epic and amazing, they feel disjointed from one other, as if each does exist in the same universe, but rather, in different dimensions (hence the Infinite Earths). Marvel, on the other hand, has no qualms about mixing characters from different groups and different comics. They also have the advantage of existing and protecting cities that are real. Unlike DC's Metropolis and Gotham, Marvel characters such as Spider-Man and Daredevil fight crime in buildings and locations that can be visited in our own reality. This creates a sense of truth to their fight. That real-world need for justice reaches more individuals and makes them feel more connected to the world they live in and the traumas they've experienced.

Soon after publishing that first guide, I received emails and messages with lists and attachments of other comics to read that discussed the sexual abuse Peter Parker (Spider-Man) endured as a child. James Atkison of the Center for Superheroes in Texas, a center specializing in help for children who have suffered childhood sexual abuse, also sent a digital copy of the origin of Bruce Banner (Hulk). Other survivors reached out with similar comic recommendations and help just when I seemed to meet dead ends in my research. While spending time investigating the complicated, interwoven Marvel universe, I began to have recollections from my own childhood, such as how I would go to my neighbor's house after school, and stay there until my mother got off work. My grandparents lived in Alabama, so my neighbors, Roy and Ms. Della, somewhat became surrogate grandparents. Ms. Della taught me to say *yes ma'am*, and *no ma'am*, while Roy taught me the value and capability of having a healthy relationship with an older Black male.

Each afternoon, when the dismissal bell sounded from Woodrow Wilson Elementary School, Roy would be waiting outside. Together, we would walk down the street to their house. Once inside, Ms. Della would prepare a bowl of chicken noodle soup and a glass of lemonade. Afterward, she would turn on the small television in the kitchen where channel 13, Fox Kids Network, would play episodes of *Batman: The Animated Series*, *Spider-Man*, and *X-Men*. During these few hours after school, I felt safe as I escaped into the world of the cartoons I loved. As an adult, I still return to Amazon Prime to watch these shows and remember the feeling of safety they provided. Now, more than ever, male survivors of childhood sexual abuse need to have a means to feel the safety and sureness provided by the heroes they loved.

Over the past few years, the "Me Too" movement has allowed survivors of sexual abuse and harassment in the workplace to come forward and let their stories be heard. Abusers such as Harvey Weinstein, Jeremy Piven, Louie C.K., Dustin Hoffman, and Matt Lauer were called out for their sexual misconduct and sexual assault. The movement has spanned from the backlots of Hollywood to the desks of NPR. However, although the "Me Too" movement has successfully removed men who abused their power for years, the overwhelming majority of individuals who have come forward to report abuse are women. In no way am I implying that this is a bad thing. In fact, the time for abusers to be held accountable for their actions is long overdue. Women and girls who have been abused have either not been believed or have been ignored for decades. It is because of the success of this movement that sexual predators like Larry Nassar and the individuals who kept him in a position capable of abusing over 150 women and girls for decades, have been put behind bars, removed from their positions of power. And yet, the conversation is still too one-sided.

Over seventy individuals have been brought down by the "Me Too" movement, yet only one was a woman. And although many women came forward to report their sexual abuse, few men brought their stories of sexual abuse and harassment to light. The traumas male survivors brought forward were often overshadowed by information pertaining to their abuser. This means that although the "Me Too" movement is a revolutionary movement that has given a voice to silenced and sexually abused women, men and boys who have been sexually abused (especially if abused by a female) have been made to feel this movement does not, and cannot, belong to them. While one in four women will be sexually abused in their lifetime, one in six males will also be sexually abused in their lifetime. Ignoring or refusing to pay attention to this startling fact leaves men and young boys vulnerable to perpetrators and perpetuates the stereotype that men and boys cannot be raped or sexually abused. This stereotype makes victims, no matter the gender, feel powerless and without options.

Understand, I am not a therapist. However, I am a male survivor of childhood sexual abuse. The information in this guide is what I have learned through reading, research, and experience while on my own journey of healing. My goal with this guide is to let other male survivors know that they are not alone in their sexual abuse. It is also to help them understand the coping mechanisms they may have used, and may still be using, so that they can move forward in their healing.

While this book can help you move toward becoming the person you wish to be, true healing cannot be accomplished on your own. Although the healing exercises are useful, they should be completed with the help of a qualified therapist or counselor who specializes in helping survivors of childhood sexual abuse. While this guide can be used to help any survivor of childhood sexual trauma, I specifically address males throughout the text. This is to provide resources for male survivors where few if any exist. While helping all survivors is critical, a key step to healing is to know the trauma you have suffered is not unique to only you, so that you can recognize yourself in the story of another. Superheroes provide a safe means for males to explore their sexual abuse and trauma. This is an opportunity for men to see themselves in the heroes and villains of the Marvel universe they grew up loving.

This volume of *Heroes, Villains, and Healing* is designed slightly differently than its predecessor. In the previous DC guide, the heroes and villains essentially had their own chapters. Unlike the DC universe, the Marvel universe is intertwined, so this guide moves through the healing process using both heroes and villains in the same chapter to help male survivors understand their coping mechanisms, the effects their childhood trauma had on themselves, and the world in which they live.

PART ONE

THE CALL TO HEALING:
Understanding the emergency stage and making the decision to heal

The idea of using superheroes to help heal childhood sexual abuse and maltreatment is not new. In fact, it has been attempted more than a few times in the past. In the 1980s, numerous artists, therapists, and counselors worked together to produce a line of comics that featured the heroes boys and girls loved, facing and dealing with childhood abuse similar to their own. Their goal then was the same as mine now: to let survivors know they are not alone. However, what they did not provide is a guide toward healing and overcoming the childhood abuse. It's not that they did not want to help in that way; it's that research was limited, and there was a void in helpful resources. This is evident in the free *Spider-Man and*

Power Pack[1] 1984 comic. The comic begins with a letter to the reader.

The letter is written by Anne H. Cohn D.P.H., who was the Executive Director of the National Committee for the Prevention of Child Abuse at the time. The letter is remarkable and empowering, not only because it provides children with a definition of child sexual abuse, but also because it emphasizes that sexual abuse can come from strangers and people they know and love. Cohn tells children who picked up this comic to not feel afraid or ashamed when she states, "it's not your fault — you can say no— and there is help out there. Just like Spider-Man and Power Pack, you are not powerless." This simple letter helped children who have been sexually abused to know they are not alone while providing the courage to heal.

After the letter, Peter Parker is shown in a makeshift darkroom in his bathroom developing pictures of himself battling a villain as the superhero, Spider-Man. While developing the images, Peter hears voices of a little boy, Tony, and his babysitter, Judy, in the apartment next door. Peter listens as Judy says, "What happened here tonight is our little secret! And you better not tell, or I may have to hurt you or get you into big trouble!"[2] Tony snivels and agrees.

It's impressive that Tony appears to be eight or nine years old, while Judy appears to be well into her teens, debunking the belief that little boys cannot be raped by a female. This sends boys the message that they can and do become sexually abused by both males and females.

The comic continues with Peter Parker putting on his mask to become Spider-Man and crawling out the window to Tony's

1. Allen, Salicrup, Mooney,
2. Allen, Salicrup, Mooney,

apartment. Judy looks out the window and sees Spider-Man, then runs out the door. Once inside, Spider-Man asks Tony what happened. Reluctantly, Tony explains how Judy said he could watch *Star Wars* only if he took off all his clothes. He tells Spidey how he did not want to take off his clothes, so he said he was going to bed. Unfortunately, Judy would not take no for an answer. Blocking the doorway to his room, Judy would not let the boy pass and began touching him.

Afterward, Tony asks Spider-Man if it was his fault. The superhero tells the boy he did nothing wrong and proceeds to tell Tony of his own childhood sexual abuse. He tells Tony the story of how he was bullied as a little boy. Because of being bullied, he spent a lot of time in the library. There, in the library, Peter met an older boy named Skip. The two spent a lot of time together, talking, hanging out, and playing pool.

One day, Peter was alone with Skip in Skip's room and Skip gave Peter a *Girlie* magazine. He then said, "Come on, Einstein! Let's conduct a little experiment of our own! Let's see if we can touch each other like the people in the magazine." Peter feels uncomfortable and tells Skip *no*, but he feels too afraid to leave. Days later, Peter told his Aunt May and Uncle Ben what happened to him.

After telling the story to Tony, Spider-Man takes Tony to his parents who are across town at a party. When they arrive, Tony tells his parents what happened with Judy. Afterward, Tony's mother says, "I'm so proud of you Tony!"[3]

The father, full of sadness for his son, says "Thanks for telling us, Tony!" The young boy snuggles into his mother's arms as his father shows true concern. Everyone thanks Spider-Man as he exits through the open window.

---

3. Allen, Salicrup, Mooney,

The comic ends with Spider-Man swinging throughout the city and reflecting on the incidents that had transpired. High above the city, he says to himself:

> *I've never admitted it to myself before, but for years I've been haunted—ashamed of that part of my past! Like Tony, I thought I did something wrong! That I was responsible! It wasn't until tonight, and Tony's similar experience, that I finally truly realized that what happened back then wasn't my fault! It really wasn't my fault! And I owe it all to Tony!*[4]

If only healing from childhood trauma were that easy. Unfortunately, it is not, and that's the primary problem with the comic. Although it does an excellent job of letting other male survivors know they are not alone in their abuse, it does not provide a realistic expectation of what may happen leading up to, during, and after disclosure. Telling others of the childhood sexual abuse (especially if the sexual abuse was at the hands of a family member or close family friend) may result in disbelief, rejection, or isolation rather than the affirmation of a loving hug that Tony experienced. Instead, individuals you disclose your abuse to may not believe the abuse occurred, or they may even side with the abuser.

Another aspect of the comic that may do more harm than good for male survivors of sexual abuse is the expectation that healing is as simple as telling your story one time to one person. Spider-Man coming to the realization that it was not his fault after telling his story for the first time is not a realistic expectation of what it means to continuously move through

---

4. Allen, Salicrup, Mooney,

the stages of the healing process. It often takes time and repetition to feel less ashamed of yourself and the abuse you suffered.

Addressing the shame and embarrassment after years of secrets takes work and patience, but it can be done. Individuals who suffer childhood sexual abuse must know that this process takes time and patience. The stages of healing cannot be checked off a list. They'll be addressed and revisited many times as each stage overlaps and merges with others, muddying the waters of where one stage ends and the other begins.

CHAPTER ONE

Understanding the Healing Process and Trauma

Before continuing to read this guide, you may be wondering, "Was I sexually abused as a child?" Answering this question is difficult, painful, and possibly confusing. To get to an answer you may want to ask yourself the following questions.

When I was a boy or young man was I:

- Fondled, kissed, or held for an adult's sexual pleasure?
- Forced to perform oral sex?
- Raped or penetrated?
- Made to watch sexual activities?
- Forced to participate and listen to excessive talk about sex?
- Forced to participate in unnecessary medical treatments that satisfied an adult's sexual needs. (An example of this would be needlessly checking genitals during a physical exam or needless removal of clothing.)
- Shown pornography?

- Forced to pose for sexual photographs?
- Forced into child prostitution or pornography?
- Forced to take part in ritualized abuse in which you were physically, psychologically, or sexually tortured?

If you answer yes to any of the questions above, you are a male survivor of childhood sexual abuse. If you did not answer yes to any of those questions but know someone who has, then this book and this information may be of use to them.

It is also important to understand that this book is not meant to be read in a single sitting. If a section of the book you are reading becomes too difficult to continue, put the text on hold until you are ready to continue and discuss what you are feeling with your therapist/counselor. Although the healing exercises are spread throughout the entire book, for easy access they have been gathered into the final section of this guide. It is my hope that this guide, like its predecessor, helps male survivors heal from their childhood trauma and know they are not alone.

Understanding the Healing Process

The healing process is unique for everyone. This is because no two individuals are the same, and so no two sexual abuses are the same. The primary purpose of this guide is to help male survivors move through the path of healing from their sexual abuse so they don't have to deny that it ever took place. By using superheroes and villains of the Marvel universe, we can discuss a topic that many men (and much of society) view as either taboo or nonexistent.

The healing process is not a straight line that allows survivors to move from start to finish in a set amount of time. When attempting to understand the brain and the effects of trauma, there is no definite beginning, middle, or end. However, there are identifiable landmarks that can assist in guiding the healing process. Research has revealed that there are thirteen steps in the process of healing from childhood sexual abuse. The thirteen steps are:

- The decision to heal
- The emergency stage
- Remembering
- Believing it happened
- Breaking the silence
- Understanding it wasn't your fault
- The child within
- Grieving
- Anger
- Disclosures and truth-telling
- Forgiveness
- Spirituality
- Resolution and moving on (Courage to Heal, 1988)

However, some survivors never experience two of the previously mentioned steps of the healing process: forgiveness and spirituality.

Moving through the thirteen steps takes time and requires each step to be continuously revisited at different stages as the survivor has different insights about himself, the life he is living, and the abuse he suffered. Healing cannot take place overnight and cannot be approached as a task that needs to be accomplished. The body and mind progress toward healing at their own pace.

Over the course of this journey, life will not come to a stop, because healing does not take place in a vacuum. This means jobs must be maintained, children must have parents, and other responsibilities must be met. This creates setbacks, relapses, and a need to revisit stages of the healing process that you thought you'd already moved through.

Because healing from childhood sexual abuse is an extremely personal journey, your healing process will be different from any other survivor's journey. Thus, in addition to offering writing exercises that allow you time to reflect and heal from the effects of the abuse, I will also include my own journey through this process, to help you feel supported and guided, and to remind you that you are not alone.

As stated previously, researchers have found thirteen steps that survivors of childhood sexual abuse go through in their journey toward healing. In my own process, I have been aided by a therapist, psychiatrist, and medication for nearly ten years. Over that time, I have discovered that many of the steps I experienced occurred simultaneously rather than separately. You may find that your journey is similar.

Many view the healing process like a highway with thirteen separate cities along the way, and a large span of miles, where life happens between each city. When a city is reached, survivors believe all they must do is refill the gas, get food, and stop to see the sights before moving on to the next destination, and that by carrying on this way, they'll reach their new home at the end of a long drive. But that's not how it works. Rather, the process is more like a river. Sometimes this river is large and peaceful. Other times, it's slim and rough. It contains rapids and lulls, and it branches into many smaller streams that flow back into one another. Sometimes these smaller streams can lead out into open ocean, complicating and confusing the journey, causing the voyager to get lost and revisit locations multiple times before returning to the correct path to make their way to their new home.

The parts of this book represent the complicated and confusing nature of this process. However, rather than thirteen separate chapters that represent the thirteen steps of the healing process, *Heroes, Villains, and Healing* combines some stages of the healing process with others and uses the monomyth of the Hero's Journey as a model for a survivor's journey of healing.

In Joseph Campbell's 1949 book *The Hero with A Thousand Faces*, the author explores the similarities of hero myths and legends across the world and throughout the ages. Campbell makes the argument that all heroes have the same defining characteristics, which mark their progression through the voyage he calls "The Hero's Journey." The hero's progress can be mapped step-by-step in the stories of Jesus Christ, Harry Potter, and even *Star Wars*. This guide uses a similar version of Campbell's Hero's Journey, but with Marvel heroes and villains, to explain the path caregivers take when they are helping people heal from childhood sexual abuse. There are five stages of the Hero's Journey that will be discussed throughout this book, and these, along with the help of a counselor or therapist trained in childhood sexual abuse, can help you explore the nature of your trauma. These stages are:

1. The Call to Healing: Understanding the Emergency Stage and Making the Decision to Heal
2. Crossing the Threshold: Remembering and Believing It Happened
3. Road of Trials: Grieving, Anger, Understanding It Was Not Your Fault, and Forgiveness
4. Transformation: Disclosures, Truth-telling, and Break-

ing the Silence

5. Master of Two Worlds: Resolution, Moving On, and Post-Traumatic Growth

As stated previously, the healing process has no definitive beginning, middle, and end. This means this guide does not have to be read from beginning to end. It should be read slowly, so you have time to explore your thoughts, develop understanding, and find healing from the specific trauma caused by childhood sexual abuse. Take your time. This is not a race. Start at a section you believe you are ready to handle; put the book down for a while if it has become particularly difficult to read. Return only when you know you are ready. Finally, as the author, I have experienced childhood sexual abuse, but I am not a trained therapist, counselor, or psychiatrist. I have not been trained to address and manage trauma and mental health in the same way they have. However, just as Peter B. Parker and all the other Spider-People attempt to help Miles Morales learn to become his own hero in the motion-picture *Spider-Man: Into the Spider-Verse*, I hope you'll use these pages and my journey as a blueprint toward developing your own definition of what it means to be a survivor. Allow the lessons of these marvelous superheroes and villains to help you begin your healing process, so you can overcome the effects of your abuse and become your own hero.

You are not alone, so do not attempt this process alone. You are, and can be, more.

CHAPTER TWO

Heroes and Villains vs. Survivors and Victims

The culture of our society is one that idolizes fictional superheroes and villains. Superheroes have moved from the realm of counterculture to popular culture, and characters such as Black Panther and Groot have become household names. This is partly why, as a survivor of childhood sexual abuse, you may see the personality traits you've adopted to survive and understand your abuse reflected in the heroes you love and the villains you love to hate.

For example, some habits and beliefs you have developed as a male survivor may have allowed you to excel and succeed in life. Think of the intellect of Charles Xavier of the X-Men and the inventiveness of Reed Richards of the Fantastic Four. These traits helped cement these characters' reputations as heroes, destined to help save humanity from the heinous actions of those bent on destroying the world, rather than as villains written off as a dangerous mutant and a superpowered freak. Unfortunately, in the same way the uncontrollable rage of Bruce Banner as the Hulk and the deceptiveness of Loki cause them to oscillate between being heroes in need of praise and menaces in need of banishment, some of the traits you have developed to cope with childhood sexual trauma may fall more in line with the habits and beliefs of villains, than with those of heroes.

However, as a survivor of childhood sexual abuse, it is important to know that the world is not a comic book. There are no superheroes or evil villains. Both archetypes are flawed and wrong. Hence why this guide will recognize flaws in the coping strategies of villains *and* heroes. We'll analyze both as you move from understanding your childhood sexual abuse toward healing. Before doing this, we need to have a shared understanding of the differences between heroes and villains. To begin, we will examine one character's journey toward becoming a hero: Spider-Man in *Amazing Fantasy #15*; and one character's path to becoming a villain: J. Jonah Jameson after he created Scorpion.

Spider-Man and Choosing to Become a Hero

Peter Parker and Spider-Man are two of the most popular characters in the Marvel universe. Although many know their names, few know how high school science-nerd Peter Parker achieved powers to become the wall-crawling, web-slinging superhero so many have come to love. Many know the big and small screen depictions of his origin story, since the story has been told and retold in movies such as *Spider-Man* (1977) (2002), *The Amazing Spider-Man* (2012), *Spider-Man: Homecoming* (2017), and in cartoons such as *Spider-Man: The Animated Series (1994-1998)*. However, it was in *Amazing Fantasy #15* (1977), that Spider-Man was born to the world.

In this comic book, nerdy, glasses-wearing, sweater-vest donned Peter Parker is presented to the reader as being less than popular. While excellent at science and loved by his guardians (Aunt May and Uncle Ben), he is ostracized by his high school classmates at every opportunity. When Peter asks for a date, he is met with, "Peter for the umpteenthtime, you're just not my type, not when dream boats like Flash Thompson are around." When attempting to make friends they say, "You stick to science, son! We'll take the chicks!" "See you around, bookworm!" and "Give our regards to the atom-smashers, Peter!" Being bullied and seen as nothing more than a science geek affects Peter's attitude, outlook, and behavior. Rather than remain kind, he grows angry, as depicted when he sniffles back a few tears and makes his way to the science exhibit, saying, "Someday I'll show them. Someday they'll be sorry! — Sorry that they laughed at me!"[5]

At the science exhibit, Peter is among other scientists all of whom are much older than him. He is watching a demonstration of radioactive rays and their possible applications. A small spider, unobserved by everyone including Peter, descends into the radioactive beam, absorbing the full transmission of radiation. The spider bites Peter moments before it dies, and immediately, Peter knows something has changed. He soon learns that he can climb walls, bend metal, and jump higher than he ever believed possible. He has become a human spider. From that moment forward, Peter will never be the same. His life is irrevocably changed in the same way that the trauma of childhood sexual abuse irrevocably changes the way you view and interact with the world. Although Peter develops superpowers and abilities that may appear to be a blessing to us, he still has

5. Lee, Ditko, *Amazing Fantasy #15*.

to learn how to use his new abilities within a society that has not been bitten by a radioactive spider. You had to do the same thing following childhood sexual abuse.

Normally in comic books, especially those of the golden and bronze age, this is the moment of the story when the protagonist decides to use his powers for good, to protect the weak, and to defend those who cannot defend themselves. However, this thought never crosses Peter's mind, and this is where Spider-Man differs from other comic-book characters. Rather than making the decision to use his powers to become a hero, Peter decides to use his newfound abilities selfishly. After all, why should he look out for others when no one has looked out for him or treated him kindly? Peter decides instead to make a little extra money as a professional wrestler. Wearing a baggy shirt and a white-clothed mask to cover his face, he steps into the ring to win one hundred dollars. He knows he's a shoe in. After winning handily, a producer approaches Peter and offers him the opportunity to perform on television. Peter agrees. Peter's actions are clearly not those of a hero; they fall more in line with a villain. However, later in the comic, a tragedy befalls the soon-to-be hero, transforming his intentions and the ways he uses his new abilities.

The comic continues with Peter perfecting his approaching television début by designing a red and blue costume that resembles a spider and has devices that fit on his wrists and shoot super-strong, thin webbing. Peter puts on the costume, calls himself Spider-Man, and performs for the cameras. Afterward, he is offered contracts that would make him rich and famous. Instead of signing them, Peter (while still wearing his Spider-Man costume) tells everyone to contact his agent. Peter is pleased with himself and his new power. He relaxes, but as he does so, a thief runs past him followed by a police officer. The officer yells to Spider-Man, asking him to help stop the perpetrator. But Spiderman does nothing and the thief gets away. When the police asked why he did not help, Peter responds, "Sorry, pal! That's not my job! I'm thru being pushed around —by anyone! From now on I just look out for number one— that means — me!" With these words, Peter feels proud of himself and the fact that no one will step on him again, no matter what.

Unfortunately, in the next few days, Peter arrives home from school to find police cars outside Aunt May and Uncle Ben's house. The police officer tells Peter that his Uncle Ben was shot, murdered by a burglar. Peter asks where the burglar has gone and is told the burglar has been trapped at the Acme Warehouse on the other side of town. Peter is angry, confused, and vengeful. He quickly changes into Spider-Man to take justice into his own hands. Spider-Man arrives and unmasks the burglar, realizing that it is the same thief he let go days prior at the television studio. Peter soon realizes, "My fault —All my fault! If only I had stopped him when I could have! But I didn't— and now —Uncle Ben— is dead…" After delivering the murdering thief to the police, Peter walks home filled with guilt and the realization that with "great power there must also come —great responsibility!"

Amazing Fantasy #15 demonstrates that traumatic childhood experiences, such as being bullied, or the death of a family member, can alter an individual's understanding of reality and can shape their subsequent interactions with the world. This comic is amazing in its ability to demonstrate the good and poor decisions that can be made following a traumatic childhood experience. In the same way Peter must learn the scope of how he has changed, you must learn how your interaction and understanding of the world is different from those who have not been victimized. Although childhood sexual abuse is not the same as developing the web-slinging abilities of Spider-Man, like Spider-Man, the new way you navigate the world can be used for good. This is the key difference between what it means to be a victim versus a survivor. Throughout the comic, science-loving Peter is bullied by his peers. He feels powerless and weak. But Peter holds himself accountable, and this is what drives him to be Spider-Man. In the same way, holding yourself accountable should be a driving force behind your actions.

The birth of Spider-Man helps to differentiate the path of a survivor from that of a victim who becomes a perpetrator. Peter Parker made the decision to become a hero in the same way you, as a male survivor of childhood sexual abuse, must make the decision to heal. If you do not, there is the potential to move from victimization to perpetration. Just think of James Jonah Jameson's hand in creating Scorpion to defeat the hero he hates, Spider-Man.

J. Jonah Jameson and Becoming a Villain

In *The Amazing Spider-Man #20*, "The Coming of the Scorpion!" readers are given the first appearance of the villain, Scorpion, and a newfound understanding of how much J. Jonah Jameson hates Spider-Man. In the previous nineteen issues of *The Amazing Spiderman*, Lee and Ditko developed the storyline of J. Jonah Jameson, editor-and-chief of *The Daily Bugle*, hating Spider-Man. Throughout the comic, Jameson writes numerous articles in which he calls Spider-Man a public menace. Why Jameson hates Spider-Man has not been made clear, especially since Spider-Man saved the life of Jameson's son. However, in this issue, Jameson does more than print false stories about the web-slinging hero; he takes matters into his own hands and attempts to have Spider-Man killed.

In this issue, J. Jonah Jameson wishes there was someone stronger than Spider-Man that he could hire to defeat the "masked menace." That gives him the idea to contact Dr. Farley Stillwell, a local scientist who had found a way to create artificial mutations in animals. Jameson and Mac Gargan, his man-for-hire, make their way to see Dr. Stillwell. Upon entering the laboratory, Jameson offers to pay Stillwell $10,000 to experiment on a human in an attempt to give them powers greater than those of Spider-Man. After a little prodding, Stillwell agrees. Moments later, he begins to experiment on Gargan in an attempt to give him the abilities of a scorpion. Stillwell warns Gargan that the experiment has the potential to affect the brain, but the man for hire says he couldn't care less about the effects as long as he gets his $10,000.

On the first attempt, the experiment is a success—sort of. Gargan is given the proportional strength of a scorpion and fitted with a mechanical tail that he can control with his thoughts. Jameson believes it was the best $20,000 he ever spent. Quickly, Jameson and the newly christened Scorpion leave to find Spider-Man. Unfortunately, Stillwell does not immediately realize that Gargan's evil nature will increase with his strength. Upon the discovery, Stillwell creates an antidote for Gargan's super strength and leaves to find the villain before it is too late to reverse the effects. Stillwell's actions are reflective of perpetrators who may later regret their actions of assault and seek redemption. However, the damage has already been done. Stillwell cannot take back the impact he has had on Gargan's transformation into the Scorpion. This mirrors how perpetrators cannot take back what they did when they caused your transformation following their victimization.

Meanwhile, on the other side of town, Scorpion defeats Spider-Man in battle. Scorpion believes that the city is now his for the taking. He decides he couldn't care less about Jameson's promised $10,000 since he no longer has to take orders from anyone. Scorpion robs an armored truck. Jameson panics, realizing his grave mistake and the possible consequences. Dr. Stillwell, still worried about more than just himself, searches the streets and finds Scorpion. He attempts to convince Scorpion to take the serum and transform back into Gargan before it is too late and he loses all sense of right and wrong, but the new villain refuses. Dr. Stillwell remains accountable for his actions. As Scorpion climbs a nearby building, Stillwell says, "No! You've got to take this! I can't live with the knowledge that I'm responsible for you!"[6] These are Stillwell's final words as he falls to his death in his attempt to follow Scorpion up a nearby building.

Stillwell had a hand in creating Scorpion. He'd have to live with this. Perpetrators, no matter how remorseful, must live with their actions as well. But Gargan's choices and actions are what define him as the villain, not Stillwell's involvement in developing him. This is true for you as well. Your choice to heal from the effects of childhood sexual abuse determine whether you continue down the path of being a victim or learn the skills needed to become a survivor.

Jameson hears of Dr. Stillwell's death, Scorpion's robbery, and the police search for the villain, and he begins to panic. He states, "I'm the one to blame! If not for me, there would be no Scorpion! Just to satisfy my own personal hatred I tried to destroy Spider-Man! And, in so doing, I've unleashed a far

6. Lee, Ditko, *The Amazing Spider-Man* #20.

worse menace upon the world! A menace I can no longer control!"[7]

To protect his identity as Mac Gargan, Scorpion plans to kill Jameson. He enters *The Daily Bugle* and attacks the editor-in-chief, but Spider-Man comes to Jameson's aid. Jameson cheers for his enemy, Spider-Man, knowing his defense is the only way Jameson will escape with his life and protect the secret of his involvement in creating the new supervillain. Spider-Man rips the artificial tail from Scorpion's body and knocks him unconscious, defeating the villain. Jameson thinks to himself, "My secret is safe...for now! But what supreme irony! I was saved from a menace whom I myself helped to create...saved by the one he was created to destroy!"[8]

Unfortunately, rather than learning from his mistakes, holding himself accountable, and giving Spider-Man credit for defeating the villain, Jameson publishes an article in *The Daily Bugle* in which he is the hero who single-handedly captured the Scorpion. With his last words in the comic, Jameson denies any sense of fault. He says:

> I know that anyone with too much power is liable to turn into a menace sooner or later! And Spider-Man is no exception! It's still my duty to fight him...to expose him...and someday to destroy him! And I will if it takes the rest of my life, I will![9]

Perpetrators survive and thrive in the realm of secrets, lies, and manipulation. Just as J.J. Jameson does everything in his

---

7. Lee, Ditko,
8. Lee, Ditko,
9. Lee, Ditko,

power to conceal his involvement in the creation of the Scorpion, including painting Spider-Man as the villain, perpetrators gaslight victims into believing the abuse was their own fault. Healing from the effects of abuse may not expose a perpetrator's lies, but it will give you strength to reject their manipulation.

Jameson, Gargan, and Dr. Stillwell all offer unique interpretations of villain, hero, blame, and accountability. Unlike Peter Parker in *Amazing Fantasy #15*, Jameson learns no lesson from his past mistakes. Instead, he remains stuck in his ways and begins to venture down the path of villain and perpetrator by refusing to hold himself accountable for his actions. He views Scorpion and Spider-Man as the only villains. He blames them for their encounters, without acknowledging his own hand in negatively impacting others. Contrarily, Dr. Stillwell takes complete accountability for his actions in unleashing an evil villain on the world. The doctor passes away while attempting to make amends. He displays the determination it may take to right past wrongs and move away from being a victim or perpetrator toward becoming a survivor.

As a male survivor of childhood sexual abuse, becoming a villain and losing control of yourself in the same way Gargan lost control of himself to become Scorpion may be one of your greatest fears. Unfortunately, without proper healing, this fear has the potential to become a reality. This means that given enough time and damaging thoughts following the sexual abuse, you could progress from being victimized to viewing yourself as a victim incapable of becoming a survivor.

Victim vs. Survivor

Understanding the abuse you have suffered means understanding the nature of the abuse *and* understanding what and how you define who you were, what you are, and who you wish to become. The title of this guide is *Heroes, Villains, and Healing*. This title implies that our reality has good guys and bad guys, heroes and villains. But things aren't this simple. The stories we read, tell, watch, and create are told with a protagonist on one side and an antagonist on the other. However, the lives we live are filled with ordinary human beings who are simultaneously capable of greatness and God-awful atrocities. The people we are, and the individuals around us, are all capable of being saints and sinners at any given moment. All of us, no matter who we are or where we come from, have something which frightens us, someone or something we love, and someone or something we've lost. The objective of this book is not to point fingers and identify as either a villain or a hero. Both are flawed. The objective is to help you understand the nature of the abuse you suffered as a child, and how to heal from its repercussions to become a complete individual who lives in the present.

Although there are no heroes and villains, there are perpetrators, victims, and survivors of childhood sexual abuse. Many perpetrators of sexual abuse were once victims of sexual abuse themselves. This does not mean all victims of sexual abuse go on to become perpetrators. According to Rape, Abuse, and Incest National Network (RAINN), most male victims of childhood sexual abuse do not go on to become perpetrators. Although perpetrators can very easily be viewed as villains, they are also often victims and survivors. This does not excuse their sexual assault or harassment of others. Each individual is responsible for their own healing. It is also important to recognize that although every survivor was a victim

of sexual abuse, every victim is not a survivor. There is a difference between the two.

Being a survivor of childhood sexual abuse, whether male
or female, does not simply mean you lived through it—that
you were not killed during or immediately following the abuse.
To be a survivor means to heal, or to work towards healing, to
become a complete individual. This does not mean suppressing
or dissociating from memories and knowledge of the horrific
events of the past but rather putting in time and effort to face
these demons. Victims blame others (including themselves) for
the problems and unfortunate events that have happened in
their life, while survivors hold each person (including themselves) accountable for their own actions, including the positive and negative repercussions of their actions. To be a survivor
is difficult, while remaining a victim can be easy.

CHAPTER THREE

Norrin Radd and Understanding the Emergency Stage

In *Silver Surfer #1*,[10] readers learn the origins of the gleaming silver rider of the cosmos known as the Silver Surfer and how he used to be known as Norrin Radd from the planet Zenn-La. Unlike the other denizens of Zenn-La, Norrin was a dreamer. Refusing to remain complacent living a life of leisure, he looked to the stars and the past to understand the prospects for the future.

Norrin's planet, Zenn-La, was scientifically advanced in every way. No one was in want of anything. In every way it was a utopia, but not for Norrin. Instead, he longed for days when his people were adventurous and looked toward the stars, rather than living a life with his feet firmly planted on the ground.

---

10. Lee, Colan, *Silver Surfer #1*.

In true comic book fashion, our protagonist, Norrin Radd, is presented with a conflict that eventually leads to a fulfillment of his longing to travel the cosmos, but at the cost of his soul. Galactus, a "Devourer of Worlds," is a being as old as the universe itself. His power knows no limits, and he arrives in Zenn-La to consume the planet and subsist on its essence.

Knowing that Zenn-La, a planet of comfort and leisure, had no way to properly defend itself from such a colossal threat, Norrin Radd offers himself as Galactus's herald, thereby saving his own planet by searching the universe for planets the World Devourer could consume. Radd frees the colossal being from his endless search for planets rich in the resources needed to sustain his life. Galactus approves. Then, with the wave of his hand, he destroys Norrin Radd and takes his soul. In Radd's place stands the sleek, stoic, and nearly expressionless Silver Surfer.

For countless years, the Silver Surfer serves Galactus before appearing in *The Fantastic Four #48* "The Coming of Galactus."[11] Alicia Masters, girlfriend of the Fantastic Four's the Thing, helps the Silver Surfer to unlock a portion of his soul, fight Galactus, and save Earth from destruction. When the two characters meet, Alicia offers the Silver Surfer food, and rather than accept, he disintegrates her kitchen table, transforming it into pure matter. He states, "We [Galactus and himself] simply change things! We change elements into energy. The energy, which sustains Galactus! For it is only He that matters!"[12]

Soon after Silver Surfer disintegrates half of Alicia's living room, the two have a conversation about what it means to live and have life. Although the comic is from the '60s and is some-

---

11. Lee, Kirby, *The Fantastic Four #48*.
12. Lee, Kirby,

what simple in its dialogue, Stan Lee and Jack Kirby do an excellent job of writing about and visualizing what it means for victims to enter the Emergency Stage and to make the decision to heal after coming to the realization that they have been abused. In the comic, Alicia says to Silver Surfer, who is holding his stomach as if sick, "According to the radio, our entire planet is in the gravest danger! But, I have the strangest feeling that somehow you possess the power to save us!"[13] Afterward, Silver Surfer responds, "I? Defy Galactus? It is unimaginable!" His face holds an expression of shock and fear, not because he is afraid of battling Galactus, a being more powerful than himself, but because in that instant the reality he knew to be true had become false. This knowledge made him feel weak, filling him with anxiety and fear that the universe operated in black-and-white terms.

Later, when confronting Galactus, Silver Surfer realizes his soul had been altered. Silver Surfer confronts Galactus and asks why he is unable to feel guilt for his past actions.

Galactus says, "Norrin Radd was an honorable man. He would not have been capable of carrying out certain desires of mine without undergoing delicate personality alterations."[14]

Hearing this, Silver Surfer demands Galactus return his soul to its previous state. With a wave of his hand, Silver Surfer's soul is returned. Seemingly, nothing seems to have changed for the hero. Soon afterward, his hands begin to drip with blood. The blood streams to the ground, creating an ocean. The guilt of what he had done as herald to Galactus overtakes him, drowning him. As he becomes more and more overwhelmed, he says:

13. Lee, Kirby,
14. Lee, Kirby,

"An infinite river of guilt over the dead of a thousand worlds. It all becomes horrifyingly clear. My dark and terrible sins come screeching from their dungeon. They seek revenge on the psyche that so long imprisoned them. Razor sharp guilt slashes away at the comforting illusions of ego and self-delusion. My life is exposed for the sham it truly is. The mask of self-righteous virtue is torn from my face. I am forced to gaze deeply into the mirror of self-realization. All home crumbles within my desperate grasp. I am lost." [15]

As a survivor, Silver Surfer's words may sound familiar. Having been sexually abused and assaulted, you may view yourself and your actions as immoral, although you were the individual who was abused. You may believe the life you have lived is a sham, and everyone can see you as a fake. Silver Surfer's overwhelming fear, anxiety, and thoughts of being an imposter are similar to how you, a survivor, may feel when entering the **Emergency Stage.**

The Emergency Stage

As a survivor there may have been, or will be, a time when you think in the same manner as the Silver Surfer. All you'll think of is the trauma and abuse you suffered in the past. During this stage, there may be extreme uncontrolled feelings of loneliness, sadness, depression, or anxiety that cannot seem to be explained. In the same way the Silver Surfer became overwhelmed by guilt when Galactus returned the hero's soul, there may be

---

15. Lee, Kirby,

moments when you feel as if you are drowning in unwanted emotions. Many survivors discover themselves crying without warning, experiencing shame, and feeling as if everyone knows about your childhood trauma. Although this stage of the healing process can best be described as panic, there are also moments of remembering and believing that it happened that blend one thought into the other, creating feelings of insanity. At this stage, some survivors wish to commit suicide, perform self-harm, or abuse alcohol or drugs. During the Emergency Stage, there is no way to combat the memories of sexual abuse or the feeling of being anxious. Unlike thoughts that might have been controllable in the past, the Emergency Stage cannot be pushed away and ignored. The memories and feelings rise to the surface and require attention, no matter what is currently happening in your life or how inconvenient their timing may be.

During and after the Emergency Stage, memories of childhood sexual abuse may fade, return, and cause the same overwhelming feelings of shame and guilt experienced by Norrin Radd after Galactus returned his soul. These memories are different from others acquired from day to day. Nonthreatening memories can be recollected with no serious strain. However, the memories of sexual abuse have the same effects on the mind and body as other traumatic events known to cause post-traumatic stress disorder (PTSD), such as mass shootings, bombings, natural disasters, and hostage situations. The only major and devastating difference is that survivors of childhood sexual abuse cannot share the memories of their experience with fellow survivors of the same traumatic event to verify the memory's accuracy. The reason for this is that sexual abuse frequently happens in secret, behind closed doors, with the survivor being told never to tell. The secrets of sexual abuse create soldiers of a war only sexual abuse survivors are allowed to discuss. In many circumstances, the only other person knowledgeable of the abuse and capable of discussing the accuracy of these memories is the perpetrator. The inability to verify traumatic memories is why many survivors doubt they were ever truly sexually abused to begin with.

Remembering the abuse varies for each survivor. Some individuals can remember details of their abuse with little problem while remaining distant and numb to feelings. Others may remember fragments, pieces, or nothing at all. This is normal, mostly because children dissociate from their bodies during the sexual abuse to manage the pain, creating instances of traumatic amnesia.

The surfacing of these memories cannot be controlled during the emergency stage. For many survivors, memories of their sexual abuse may seem to happen without explanation, appearing in vivid dreams and nightmares. However, the flashback of memories can occur for several reasons. Some of these reasons may be:

- **Triggers**: Certain smells, touches, a familiar sound from the past, internal sensations, or visual images may trigger a flashback of a sexual abuse. These are recalled through sense memories the body has held onto even if the mind has tried to push them away.
- **Quitting Addictions**: Sometimes addictions to drugs and alcohol are coping mechanisms to deal with the trauma of childhood sexual abuse. After quitting an addiction, memories that were once repressed are now allowed to be remembered.
- **Life-Changing Events**: Some common life-changing events include becoming a parent, the death of a family

member, being robbed or vandalized, getting married, or experiencing a natural disaster such as a fire or earthquake. All of these can cause memories of childhood sexual abuse to surface.

- **Becoming Safe:** Being sexually abused as a child meant never truly feeling safe. Often, survivors may have viewed adults as individuals who could not be trusted. This meant protecting emotions and limiting access to feelings. However, as an adult, if a safe environment is created, overtime the mind and body will allow emotions to become unhindered and memories to surface.
- **Visuals:** Watching news coverage, movies, or videos may trigger memories of your own sexual abuse.

Throughout the Emergency Stage it may feel as though the memories have control over your life and who you are, rather than the other way around. However, over time, you will no longer view the memories as a curse that cause inexplicable bouts of misery and sadness. Given enough time, patience, and support from a trained counselor or therapist, the pieces of your past abuse will begin to fit together to provide understanding and healing. For the Silver Surfer, the return of his soul brought with it the memory of all the pain and destruction he was forced to endure at the hands of Galactus. However, it also returned the pleasant memories of the life he once lived on Zenn-La with the love of his life, Shalla-Bal. While difficult to endure, the painful memories of the abuse can expand to reveal pieces of a past life and pleasant memories that have been forgotten.

If you push the memories away, as may have been the practice in the past, during the Emergency Stage the memories will surface in the form of exhaustion, nightmares, depression, migraines, anxiety, and uncontrollable dissociative episodes that may take the form of vivid daydreams. Denying your mind and body access to these memories will take a toll if you do not deal with them properly.

What must be remembered with each flashback and trigger is that it will not last forever. Over time, as you progress through this stage of the healing process, you will notice the days and seasons change just as before. There is no way to fully explain the emergency stage or what may be experienced except to say it involves panic. However, there are strategies to help you get through this stage, no matter how long it takes or how often you return.

Healing Exercise #1: Creating Your Own Safe Place

In X-Men, Charles Xavier creates a school as a haven for mutants. It's a place where they are not afraid to be themselves. Here, individuals born with exceptional superhuman abilities, come to understand and control their abilities without fear of being persecuted, hurting themselves, or hurting others. This is where Professor Xavier helped Wolverine unravel the mystery of his past, come to terms with the boy he was, the monster he was created to be, and come to peace with the atrocities he committed in the past. While in the Emergency Stage, and throughout your healing journey, it is important to create a safe place to escape and heal in the same manner Charles Xavier created the Xavier Institute for Higher Learning. This is how I described a safe place as I began my healing journey:

When we were young, we had places we went to, somewhere to get away from what was bothering us, where we could sit in peace without siblings or adults having access to us. When we sat down in this place, we always felt good. It's in this place we were able to play with the objects of childhood. There, we could think our thoughts and say our words out loud, without anyone telling us, judging us, or pushing us. That was the wisdom of childhood. Now you can call on that same wisdom. Find or create a safe place for yourself now. A place just for you, not for sharing with anyone else. Your paradise. Spend scheduled time there at first. In the future, you will be drawn to your safe space naturally. There you can rest, heal, hide, think, play, and get yourself ready to go back out and be your best.

It is in this place you will learn to love yourself in the same manner that Henry "Hank" McCoy learned to accept his inner Beast. Here, you'll remember and come to terms with the reality of your traumatic past in the same manner Logan realized he is more than just Wolverine. You'll develop inner peace in the same way Storm learned to calm her inner tempest. Without this safe place, there can be no true growth and inner perseverance. It is also in this safe place you should practice mindfulness, self-care, and meditation. Science has proven that meditation helps manage poor heart rate variability which can help reduce mental health problems, depression, and PTSD. When creating your safe place, it is important that it be *physically*, *mentally*, and *emotionally* safe.

Physical Safety is when the body is no longer in danger and able to relax in the same way Hulk can transform back into Bruce Banner when the threat of danger has passed. *Mental safety* means having the ability to remain grounded, centered, and focused on your own thoughts and feelings without dissociating from reality, like how Matt Murdock as Daredevil focuses his heightened senses to prevent the many sounds and sensations of his surroundings from overwhelming him. *Emotional safety* means having the ability to control and regulate feelings without consistently experiencing hyperarousal and panic attacks, so you aren't like Juggernaut running like an out-of-control freight train, or Marc Spector losing himself inside the hero, Moon Knight.

All three of these forms of safety interact with one another, oftentimes making it difficult (or even impossible) for a survivor to differentiate between their body, mind, and emotions. Fulfilling each measure of safety requires a different set of tools that will be explored throughout this guide.

Creating a safe place is vital to your recovery because without a sense of safety and security, the work of creating a survivor's narrative to understand the nature of childhood sexual abuse is not sustainable. In fact, if a survivor does not feel safe when attempting to practice mindfulness or meditation, the practice can cause more harm than good. This is because fear is one of the primary obstacles to mindfulness. In David Treleaven's book *Trauma-Sensitive Mindfulness,* he explains how one of the worst things survivors of trauma can be forced to do is relive the horrors that have caused them so much pain. Without first placing themselves in a place of safety, survivors can force themselves to remain trapped in the Emergency Stage.

When identifying your own level of safety as a male survivor, authors Williams and Poijula explain in *The PTSD Handbook* how it is important to ask yourself eleven simple questions when attempting to gauge a sense of safety. It would be helpful to keep a journal of your responses to track how your responses either change over time or remain the same. If you feel triggered or overwhelmed when answering the questions, put this guide down and return when you are comfortable. Remember, healing is not a race but a journey. Give yourself time.

Safety Questions [16]

1. How safe is your environment? Is your home safe? Why/why not?
2. What makes you feel physically safe when you are alone? With others? In different situations?
3. Are those with whom you live or interact safe? If they are, what makes the setting and those people safe? If they are not, what makes them unsafe?
4. If you are not safe at home, is there anything you can do to increase your sense of safety?
5. If you are not safe with or around those closest to you, what will make your situation safer?
6. How can you (and how do you) protect yourself?
7. How successful are you at physically protecting yourself?
8. When are you physically the safest?
9. When do you mentally and emotionally feel the safest?
10. How can you protect yourself when you are with people you do not know?
11. What do your answers to these questions tell you about you and your sense of safety?

To assist you in becoming calm and knowing you are safe, follow the healing meditation exercises below.

Healing Exercise #2: Meditation

---

16. Williams, Poijula, *The PTSD Workbook: Simple Effective.*

A strategy that is helpful throughout all stages of the healing process is learning to meditate. Meditation allows time for thoughts to mature, the mind to rest, and the body to relax. To many, beginning to meditate seems impossible, but like all other activities it takes practice to master. To understand different meditation techniques, you may want to seek out classes, research, and watch videos on the Internet to develop this skill. As you begin this process, it is important to know that there is no goal to be reached. Instead, meditation requires a calm mind. Below are three different meditation strategies you can use:

Stairs:

Create a safe place.

While in your safe place, sit comfortably for fifteen minutes. If you feel comfortable doing so, play relaxing sounds, such as nature sounds of crashing waves or falling rain.

Close your eyes and breathe slowly. Take deep breaths in through your nose and out through your mouth.

Imagine Professor Xavier has placed the image of ten steps in your mind. He has developed these steps to be of the style you feel comfortable imagining. Now, imagine he has placed numbers on each step descending from ten at the top to one at the bottom. The color of the paint and steps is the color most pleasing to you.

Unlike the War Room, Xavier has created this space in your mind to be completely safe, allowing you to visualize yourself carefully walking backward down each step one at a time. As you descend, continue to breathe deeply in through your nose and out through your mouth. With each step, you should feel yourself becoming more at rest and your mind more at ease.

When you reach the bottom of the stairs, continue to breathe while allowing your mind to wander and unwind on its own for the remainder of the fifteen minutes. Know that you are safe, allowed to feel your emotions without judgment, and can confront painful memories without fear or anxiety.

At the end of the fifteen minutes, slowly ascend the steps until you return to your body.

Progressive Relaxation:

Create a safe place.

While in your safe place, sit comfortably for fifteen minutes. If you feel comfortable doing so, play relaxing sounds such as nature sounds of crashing waves or falling rain.

Close your eyes and breathe slowly. Take deep breaths in through the nose and out through the mouth.

Imagine you are your favorite superhero, whoever that may be. Now, as the character, very slowly, beginning at your toes, tense your muscles. Move slowly up from your feet to your calves, thighs, torso, fingers, arms, shoulders, neck, and head. Afterward, slowly begin to relax your muscles in reverse order. Start at your head, down to your neck, shoulders, arms, fingers, torso, thighs, calves, feet, and toes.

Continue to tense and relax your muscles for the remainder of the fifteen minutes (at least three to five times).

Neon Light:

Create a safe place.

While in your safe place, sit comfortably for fifteen minutes. If you feel comfortable doing so, play relaxing sounds such as nature sounds of crashing waves or falling rain.

Close your eyes and breathe slowly. Take deep breaths in through your nose and out through your mouth.

Imagine yourself as the Human Torch. As an exercise in concentration, imagine extending your flame from your body in the form of a ring of fire. The fire does not burn you. Instead, it is soothing and an extension of your body. Now, imagine the ring loosely encircling your ankles. Again, the ring does not hurt, but it has a sense of healing radiating outward, up into your skin. Slowly imagine the ring extending up your body, expanding and retracting to match the shape and form of your body as it moves all the way to your head. As it moves, imagine the warmth radiating from the glow of the ring and into your body.

Once the ring reaches your head, imagine it slowly descending down your body, healing as it does, for the remainder of the fifteen minutes.

Strategies for Surviving the Emergency Stage

Although there is no way to prevent the Emergency Stage—to keep the memories of your abuse from occurring through flashback, or to minimize the effects that no longer denying the sexual abuse will have on you—there are techniques that can help relieve the anxiety and stress of progressing through this stage of the healing process.

- **Find people you can talk to.** Create a support staff you can trust that will not judge your past or minimize your feelings. While it is important to create a safe place, you cannot spend all your time in your own private Xavier School for the Gifted during the Emergency Stage. Instead, you must venture out to live your life through this trying time.
- **Seek a counselor/therapist.** You are not alone. Do not take on the task of attempting to heal without help. Find a trained professional who specializes in sexual abuse trauma to help reassure you that the emotions and thoughts you are having are real and justified. This will provide hope and reassurance that you are not going crazy. Receiving help does not make you weak. The Avengers work together to take down evil; why can't you?
- **Seek medication.** Do not believe suffering the traumatic event of childhood sexual abuse does not include the possibility of getting help to handle overwhelming emotions and thoughts. Medication is not right for everyone, but it may help relieve symptoms of anxiety and depression, not dull them away. Consult a doctor to find out if this is a good fit.
- **Do something spiritual.** This does not have to involve

going to a church. Doctor Stephen Strange was able to discover new meaning in his life through the study of the mystic arts. Finding a healthy connection to something bigger than yourself can be beneficial for you. Later in the book, spirituality will be discussed further, but prayer, meditation, and connecting to your religion can provide strength and support when you need it.

- **Read or write a comic.** Find a hobby. Something you enjoy that is healthy and relaxes your senses. This may include working out, listening to music, watching your favorite Marvel movie, reading a comic, or playing your favorite video game. When overwhelmed, take some time to do something for yourself. Do not feel bad for having good self-care.

CHAPTER FOUR

Making the Decision to Heal

The first step of the Hero's Journey is the departure from home and familiar territory to places unknown. It is here that the hero receives the "Call to Adventure." Something occurs that requires a hero to rise up and meet a challenge. This could be the kidnapping of a princess, the rise of an ancient evil from the past, or, in the case of Spider-Man, it is when he chose not to stop the thief who would eventually kill his Uncle Ben.

In Spider-Man's first appearance, Peter is bullied by his peers. On the first page, he is pointed at and laughed at by his fellow high schoolers when they say, "Peter Parker? He's Midtown High's only professional wallflower!"[17] When attempting to invite a group of friends to the new science hall exhibit, they respond by saying, "You stick to science son! We'll take the chicks!" and "Give our regards to the atom-smashers, Peter!"[18] While walking into the science exhibit where Peter will gain his abilities as Spider-Man, Peter mumbles to himself with

17. Lee, Ditko, *Amazing Fantasy #15*.
18. Lee, Ditko,

a grimace on his face and tears in his eyes, "Some day I'll show them! Some day they'll be sorry! Sorry they laughed at me."[19]

As a survivor, you may be able to relate to Peter's sense of isolation and loneliness, believing others are unable to see the superhero beneath the surface. Unfortunately, these feelings of exclusion can transform heroes into villains and survivors into victims.

After acquiring his abilities as Spider-Man, Peter does not suddenly decide to use his abilities to fight crime. Instead, he decides to use his abilities to make money and no longer feel like the weak little science nerd everyone decides to walk over. First, he uses his abilities to win a hundred dollar cash prize to take down a professional wrestler. After the match, a TV producer offers Peter a television spot to showcase his abilities. From there, Peter shoots his first television spot as the Amazing Spider-Man, believing he is finally being respected as the marvel he knew he was all along. Peter does not stop the thief being chased by a police officer in the television studio. Instead, Peter chose to ignore the "Call to Adventure." He let the thief escape into the elevator, and tells the police officer, "Sorry, pal! That's your job! I'm thru being pushed around by anyone! From now on I just look out for number one. That means me!"[20]

A few days later, after Spider-Man has become the talk of the nation, the same thief who robbed the television studio breaks into the home of his Aunt May and Uncle Ben and kills the man who raised Peter as his son, leaving his Aunt May a widow. Peter's refusal to answer the "Call to Adventure" put events into action that led Peter to use his

19. Lee, Ditko,

20. Lee, Ditko,

abilities to fight crime as the superhero, Spider-Man, rather than to become a television sensation. Survivors must make a similar decision. Rather than answering a "Call to Adventure," survivors must decide whether they are going to make the "Decision to Heal," or if they'll refuse to answer the call.

As a survivor, you may believe it will be easier not to heal, to continue along the path you have journeyed for most of your life, and cope with your abuse using hypervigilance, workaholism, and perfectionism as coping mechanisms. Unfortunately, after entering the Emergency Stage, returning to the reality that existed prior to the Emergency Stage is an impossibility. Suppression of the childhood trauma may be possible for a short while, but over time, thoughts of the abuse and feelings of shame and anxiety will always return. Sometimes they come back more potently and powerfully than they were before. Refusing to make the Decision to Heal keeps survivors perpetually returning to the Emergency Stage, where they are trapped in the trauma of the past, unable to progress. Given enough time, the fear and pain of the unresolved sexual abuse will fester and mutate into rage, depression, and anxiety, transforming the survivor into a victim, hurting and bleeding on those closest to them from the unhealed wounds.

Making the Decision to Heal is not easy. It requires questioning many beliefs about the classic definition of what it means to be a man. Like the hero Vision, you'll explore vulnerability, express dormant emotions, reveal secrets that may be difficult for others to hear, and come to the realization that you are not a superhero; you are only human.

This Decision to Heal requires strength and understanding that healing will not be easy; it requires hard work. Although making the Decision to Heal may be difficult, this journey is deserving of every survivor, regardless of what may have happened prior to beginning to heal. Making the Decision to Heal is life-changing, spiritual, and deeply moving, but it is a decision no one else can make for you. It means taking back the control that was taken from you as a child. Healing allows you to become the complete person you were always meant to become.

If you have made the difficult Decision to Heal, the exercises and strategies below will help you manage your moments of anxiety.

Writing Exercise #3: Analyzing a Moment of Anxiety

It is not a matter of *if* you will have an anxiety or panic attack during the Emergency Stage, but *when*. This means being prepared when an attack occurs, knowing how to interpret the attack after it occurs, and knowing how to prevent the possibility of future attacks. To help you along the healing process and moments of high stress during the Emergency Stage, I have added a graphic organizer that can help you before, during, and after a panic attack. (A larger version is available in the Writing Exercises chapter if you would like to make copies.)

Understanding Your Panic Attack Graphic Organizers

Understanding Your Panic Attack (Before/During)		
Trigger(s):	Hero or Villain	Emotions

Identify the trigger which led to the panic attack, the location where it occurred, and what occurred during the attack.	Does this attack identify more with a hero or villain? If you can, identify a character or a scene in a comic or movie which seems to relate.	Which emotions seem to be the strongest during the attack? This may require using the attached emotion chart.

Understanding Your Panic Attack (After)		
Becoming Safe	Beliefs About Self and Sexual Abuse	Strategy for Future
What did you do to relieve the anxiety and become safe? Was it effective? What could you have done differently?	What new memories or beliefs about yourself and your abuse do you now have after the panic attack?	What can you do in the future to help prevent this attack from occurring or to lessen its effects.

To assist you in understanding how to use these graphic organizers properly, I will use them to analyze Peter Parker's moments of high anxiety and stress in *Spider-Man #24* "Spider-Man Goes Mad."

Spider-Man Goes Mad

In *The Amazing Spider-Man #24* Peter Parker believes that his superpowers have driven him crazy. The comic begins with Dr. Ludwig Rinehart visiting J. Jonah Jameson at the offices of *The Daily Bugle*. He tells Jameson,

"I am here on vacation from Europe! As a psychiatrist I am very interested in reading about this Spider-Man of

yours! I have handled cases similar to his! From my experience, I can say he is a very sick man! You see, he is
in a fantasy world now! He wants to be a spider…but,
of course, he is a human being! It is only a matter of
time before his Id and his Ego get so confused that he
forgets who he really is…and then he will suffer a severe breakdown."[21]

Hearing this, Jameson becomes ecstatic and calls for an immediate extra edition of *The Daily Bugle* to be printed. The
next day, Peter reads the article and becomes concerned about
his mental health. After calling *The Daily Bugle* to verify the
article is true (Jameson prints whatever he wants if it has the
possibility of bringing down Spider-Man,) Peter races to go
find Dr. Rinehart. He is afraid he may go crazy at any moment.
He changes into Spider-Man and quickly swings by *The Daily
Bugle* offices to find out where he can find the doctor. However, on the way, Spider-Man begins to hallucinate. He sees Doctor Octopus appear and disappear from a solid brick wall,
Sandman attack and dissolve beneath his feet, and Vulture attack from the air only to vanish like the other two villains.

Spider-Man lands on a nearby rooftop and begins to panic
uncontrollably. The superhero holds his head, cowers in a corner, and thinks to himself,

*I can't go to Jameson now…can't afford to be near any-
one! Can't let others see what's happening to me! And
what if it gets worse? What if I lose control completely?
What if I can't tell what's real from what's imaginary?
What if I should start attacking innocent people think-*

---

21. Lee, Ditko, *The Amazing Spider-Man* #24.

ing they're dangerous criminals? I'd have to be locked up. Put away! [22]

Peter races home, hoping all he needs is a good night's sleep, but he freaks out when he sees how white he is in the mirror. Fearing the worst, he grabs a copy of the newspaper and races out the door to find Dr. Rinehart.

As Spider-Man, Peter arrives at the doctor's house. He rings the bell and enters only to see the room upside down. Dr. Rinehart is sitting at his desk on the ceiling. He welcomes Spider-Man and says he will help the hero deal with his hallucinations as best he can. Afraid of hurting the doctor, Spider-Man runs away, believing he is beyond help. However, he sees the other rooms in the house are upside down as well, so Spider-Man decides to stay out of fear of hurting innocent people on the street.

Dr. Rinehart convinces Spider-Man to stay and be analyzed. He holds the superhero as he covers his face and tells him everything will be fine. When he uncovers Spider-Man's face, everything is right-side up. While sitting on the couch, Spider-Man believes he sees Doctor Octopus, Sandman, and Vulture, and Dr. Rinehart's assures Spider-Man that he needs psychotherapy. Spider-Man agrees and lies back on the couch.

Dr. Rinehart tells Spider-Man the root of his problem is his dual identity. He tells the superhero he must stop being Spider-Man in order to be cured. The superhero believes him, and moments before he reveals his secret identity, J. Jonah Jameson bursts through the door and tells him Dr.

---

22. Lee, Ditko,

Rinehart is a fraud. The entire plan had been schemed by the villain, Mysterio, using projections and mechanized rooms, and the comic ends with Peter walking off into the sunset with a pretty blond. (It was the '60s. What do you expect?)

To help you understand the graphic organizer, I will complete the graphic organizer as if it had been written by Peter during his moments of anxiety and panic.

Understanding Your Panic Attack (Before/During)		
Trigger(s):	**Hero or Villain**	**Emotions**
Identify the trigger which led to the panic attack, the location where it occurred, and what occurred during the attack.	Does this attack identify more with a hero or villain? If you can, identify a character or scene in a comic or movie which seems to relate.	Which emotions seem to be the strongest during the attack? This may require using an emotion chart.
• Reading an issue of *The Daily Bugle* in which Dr. Rinehart stated that Spider-Man would eventually go crazy.	• Well, obviously I'm a hero, but the fact that I was willing to give up being Spider-Man to ensure no one got hurt shows my willingness to do what needs to be done for the greater good.	• Anxiety • Fear • Loneliness • Confusion

• I was at Aunt May's house when I first read the article. Next, I called *The Daily Bugle* offices to make sure it was true. Afterward, I changed into Spider-Man and went to find Dr. Rinehart. On the way, I imagined seeing Doctor Octopus, Sandman, and Vulture, but they vanished into thin air.		
• This caused me to really panic. On top of a roof, I cowered in a corner and questioned whether I was going crazy.		

Understanding Your Panic Attack (After)		
Becoming Safe	**Beliefs About Self and Sexual Abuse**	**Strategy for Future**
What did you do to relieve the anxiety and become safe? Was it effective? What could you have done differently?	What new memories or beliefs about yourself and your abuse do you now have after the panic attack?	What can you do in the future to help prevent this attack from occurring or to lessen its effects.
• To relive the anxiety, I caught the bad guy with the help of Flash Thompson and Jameson. (I never thought I would say that).	• I feel more assured now that I am meant to be Spider-Man, and that I have to do everything I can to make Uncle Ben proud.	• In the future, I need to keep an eye out for signs that Mysterio is messing with my mind.

• I did not have to jump to such quick decisions. I'm a scientist. I need to develop a hypothesis and explore all the possibilities before jumping to conclusions.		

These organizers will help you understand the triggers which lead to attacks, and they provide items to review with your trained counselor or therapist while in session. The only difference between your writing and that of Peter's (other than the fact that he has superpowers) is that you should develop a safe place where you can manage your moments of anxiety while feeling the most comfortable. Read the section below to understand how to create your own safe place.

Writing Exercise #4: Your Hero Code

Everyone has a code that they live by, even if it is never stated or written. This code guides the actions and beliefs of individuals. For some, it may change slightly over time, but if you don't understand the code and how to change it, then at its core, it will remain the same.

Your code, as a male survivor of childhood sexual abuse, may consist of absolute thoughts and black-and-white thinking. Although this worldview may have allowed you to survive your childhood trauma, as an adult this kind of thinking can lead to the transformation from becoming the hero of your own story to the villain of others' stories, in the same way that

Doctor Doom, Magneto, Galactus, Thanos, and many others attempted to justify their immorality with beliefs that their actions were for the greater good. As a child, black-and-white thinking may have provided a source of strength, but over time, such coping strategies can lose their needed effects.

Take the opportunity in your journal to explore your own hero code as you make the decision to heal. Explore your views of yourself, the world, and others with your therapist or counselor. It will allow both of you to see evidence of some form of the absolute thinking you have developed.

Over time, as you move through the healing process, your code will change. The absolute thoughts you held at the beginning of the process should change, as your brain begins to heal from the trauma of being sexually abused. When you feel you have made strides in your journey toward healing, rewrite your code. Take notice of the differences, discuss them with your therapist or counselor, and praise your achievements. No matter what, every survivor deserves to heal—even you.

Below is my hero code from the beginning of my journey. At the end of this guide, I will return to my hero code and explain how it has changed over the years as I have moved along my healing journey.

My Hero Code (Autobiographical)

- I don't need anyone's help. I can do anything and everything on my own if I really try.
- People can't be trusted to be there when you need them. Eventually, given enough time, everyone lets you down. It's best to learn not to depend on anyone in the first place.

- I don't need to rest. If I push myself, I can keep going.
- I must be happy. If I'm not happy, then I'm sad or angry. There is no middle ground.
- I have a plan and I'm sticking to it.
- If I don't keep working and moving, I am going to lose everything.
- I'm not strong enough.
- I must be strong enough.
- Everyone is depending on me.
- It's all my fault.
- I must be perfect.

PART TWO

CROSSING THE FIRST THRESHOLD:
Remembering and believing it happened

Who is Wolverine? What did his life entail before joining the X-Men? Authors Bill Jemas, Paul Jenkins, and Joe Quesada attempt to answer these questions in a six-part comic series detailing Wolverine's life before, and just after, acquiring his mutant abilities.

The series begins with *Wolverine: The Origin* #1 "The Hill." Here, readers are introduced to a young, red-headed girl named Rose O'Hara.[23] She works as a playmate and nurse for James Howlett, the young master of the estate who, though jovial, is often sickly and neglected by his mother. She also looks after a boy known as "Dog" who works on the estate while being abused by his alcoholic father, Logan. Although

23. Jemas, *Wolverine: The Origin* #1.

the three characters get along as playmates when they are young, as they grow older their relationship splinters until eventually shattering in issue #2. In *Wolverine: The Origin #2* "The Inner Child" readers witness for the first time the birth of the iconic hero many would come to know as Wolverine.[24] Here, the final image depicts James on his knees with bone claws extending from the knuckles of his hands, as he screams over the dead body of his believed-to-be father.

The series continues with James and Rose fleeing the Howlett mansion in Canada. James is unaware of who he is, what has happened to him, and what has happened to his father. Only after reaching the Klondike does Rose give James the name Logan. It's from that moment onward that James, the young jovial boy, is replaced by Logan, the gruff animalistic young man who drinks too much and spends nights hunting with a pack of wild wolves. Throughout the rest of the series, James attempts to push away the memory of what happened to him as a child and pretends the tragedy of losing his parents never occurred. He has trouble understanding and trusting his memory, and he refuses to believe it happened until the past catches up to his present and forces him to acknowledge his trauma.

Logan's loss of memory is not uncommon among survivors of childhood trauma. As a male survivor, you may have trouble remembering your past abuse in the same way Logan refuses to admit the trauma of his past. However, piecing together the memory of childhood trauma is what it means to "Cross the First Threshold" on your journey of healing. Rather than a hero beginning his training to battle monsters and save damsels in distress, survivors take on the difficult task of

---

24. Jemas, *Wolverine: The Origin #2*.

not only remembering but acknowledging that the sexual abuse occurred and has impacted their development as a human being. This part of the book helps to understand **dissociation,** how childhood sexual abuse affects memory, and what can occur if survivors **deny** that the sexual abuse occurred.

CHAPTER FIVE

The Effects of Childhood Trauma

Logan came to exist only after he witnessed the loss of his parents, was rejected by the society he had grown to love, and accidentally caused the death of his first love, Rose. The transformation of James into Logan helps to illustrate how traumatic events, such as childhood sexual abuse, can create post-traumatic stress resulting in dissociation. For some survivors, dissociation is the only way to survive and cope with the trauma of childhood sexual abuse. While this is true for James Howlett when he became Logan, a better representation of the impact of trauma on a survivor's feelings can be seen when Logan was forced to become Weapon X.

Before becoming a member of Professor Xavier's X-Men, Wolverine was known as Weapon X. In *Marvel Comics Presents Weapon X #76-84* "Weapon X", Gerod James, Simon Furwen, and Robert Campanelia explore the experiments performed on Logan to transform him into a living weapon.

These comics are drawn in the grit, detail, and gore that

only the early '90s can provide. Throughout this eight-part series, there are three main characters besides Logan: Miss Hines, the petite, short-haired N.A.S.A operative; Doctor Cornelius, the bearded overseer of Logan's vitals and physiology; and a thin, bald man with mirrored glasses known only as the Professor. These three individuals are responsible for exploiting Logan's mutant ability to heal by melding his entire skeleton with the fictional metal adamantium. Once cooled, adamantium is said to be the strongest metal on the planet. They experiment with Logan to transform him into a living weapon.

To dehumanize Logan, they do not call him by his name. They call him Weapon X. They also refuse to give him clothing, believing it is not needed if he can regenerate. These techniques, which treat him more like an animal than a man, along with surgical implants throughout his mind and body, are successful in brainwashing Logan to follow their kill orders. The series demonstrates the effects continuous exposure to trauma has on feelings. The three make Logan into an emotionless being with savage instincts whose only objective is to accomplish the given mission.

Fight, Flight, Freeze

Issue #76 demonstrates the initial effects of trauma and the three possible reactions the mind and body have to abuse and assault. In this first issue, Logan is lying in what looks to be a casket, covered from head to toe in blue, red, and yellow wires moving in, out, and around his body. Miss Hines, Doctor Cornelius, and the Professor look down at Logan from a compact room filled with monitors, dial pads, and cold metal fixtures.

Although Logan is sedated, the torment of the experiments being performed on his body causes the machines around him to
overload, and he regains consciousness. The monitors around
the room project the images and thoughts radiating from Logan's mind. He screams, "I...hurting...PAIN! WHAT HAVE
YOU DONE TO ME!!?"[25] In these images, Logan views himself with spikes extending from his skull and from his chest as
he grabs Miss Hines and demands to know what has happened
to him. Before being further sedated, the Professor calls Logan
"an animal" and the comic ends with Logan visualizing the
bloody death of the Professor.

In these images, it is clear Logan is in unbearable pain. His
body has been violated in ways he cannot understand except
in terms of torment. Those images are projected from his mind
to the monitor until there is nothing left for him to do but suc-
cumb to sedation. Logan's reaction to pain is true for anyone
facing danger and possible death. Unfortunately, after having
endured sexual abuse as boys, many adult male survivors view
themselves as animals just as Logan did. Remembering the torment of the past can cause many to seek sedation. While Logan
was sedated and continuously tortured by his experimenters,
male survivors seek sedation in healthy ways such as exercise
and unhealthy ways such as the numbing effects of drugs, alcohol, and the contemplation of suicide. The only lasting anti-
dote to lifelong sedation is to begin the healing process, and
that includes associating the memories of the past.

Dr. Stephen Porges explains in *The Polyvagal Theory* how
individuals have three possible responses to danger. The first is
social engagement. It is here that people call out for help from
those nearby. Logan experienced this first stage when he called

---

25. James, Furwen, and Campanelia, *Marvel Comics Presents Weapon X #76*.

for Miss Hines to give him answers. However, if no one comes to help, the individual enters the second stage: *fight* or *flight*. It's in this stage people either fight off their attacker or run for safety. When no one came to Logan's help he chose to fight. Unfortunately, fighting failed as well, and for the remainder of the series, Logan existed in the third and final stage. This stage is known as *freeze* or *collapse*. In this stage, the person tries to remain alive by shutting down and using as little energy as possible.

The final stage of Porges's theory is a form of dissociation where the survivor loses his ability to feel and express any emotion because feeling and expressing any emotion is too painful. Shutting down is Logan's only choice for survival, and this mirrors the way many children who find themselves unable to escape their abuse numb their emotions as the only way to survive and remain sane.

Understanding Dissociation

As a male survivor of childhood sexual abuse, you may have taught yourself that your body cannot be trusted, and that it is not safe for you to find enjoyment and feel free to live in your body. This is what James Howlett taught himself after he discovered his mutant abilities. The safety and security of living in your own body was taken away when you were sexually abused as a child. The fear of being violated again as an adult may sometimes lead you to disconnect from your body. This is called **dissociation**, and it is the ability to separate your mind from your body and the emotions you experience from coping with the pains you were forced to endure.

When you were a child, you may not have been able to physically escape your abuse, so you emotionally and psychically separated from your abuse. It gave you the ability to endure tremendous amounts of physical and psychological pain that was impossible to endure without the ability to separate your mind from your body.

The Courage to Heal states that when a survivor dissociates from their body, they:

- may not feel pleasure in physical activities
- aren't aware of messages their bodies give them
- feel numb or disconnected from physical sensations
- are often on high alert for danger
- are unable to relax or feel physically safe[26]

Although survivors can dissociate from their bodies, it is important to also understand that there are many different ways to dissociate. You may not dissociate from your body. Instead, you may dissociate either mentally or emotionally. This, too, is normal. These coping strategies may have been essential to your survival as a child. However, as an adult, dissociation can become a habit and can create problems when dealing with threatening situations. In some cases, it can lead to **dissociative identity disorder (DID)**. This occurs when there is no way to physically escape intolerable pain, so a person creates new selves or alternate personalities to separate from the abuse and withstand the trauma.

Some examples of dissociation can be seen in different issues of *Weapon X*. For example, in issue #79, Logan is stripped of all his clothing, exposed to the elements of winter, and

---

26. Bass, Davis, *The Courage to Heal.*

forced to battle and kill a pack of wolves as they rip through his flesh. After successfully saving his own life, the three leave Logan to sleep in the blood and guts of his kill while his face and actions remain absent of emotion. Later in that same issue, Logan again shows dissociation after hunting and decapitating a wild bear. In issue #78, Logan is degraded by being viewed as nothing more than a lab animal. When Logan passes out on the floor, a cup of hot coffee is poured on his face. Logan never even winces, let alone opens his eyes.

Eventually, Logan breaks free from their control and proceeds to kill everyone in the facility. However, he remains detached through each kill. He wears the same expression he had while hunting and killing animals in the wild. The killing of the people in the facility brings him neither pain nor pleasure. He is ambivalent. He has dissociated. The trauma of the pain, torture, and animalistic treatment left him numb and unfeeling, as if his mind and body were operating on autopilot.

Logan's lack of emotion and feeling may sound familiar to your own. After years of repressing feelings of fear, pain, sadness, depression, and anxiety to pretend that everything is alright, you may feel as zombie-like as Logan. The world and its events may pass you by as you feel little-to-no joy or sorrow. Each day, week, and month becomes a series of tasks to be checked off a list and completed. Like Logan, you may feel exposed to the world, hurting but unable to give words to the way you feel.

However, in issue #84, when Logan has freed himself of his abusers, he no longer dissociates. It's as if he has awoken from a nightmare. He stares at the blood on his body, wondering where it came from. He sees the dead body of Doctor Cornelius and says to himself, "I know this man. In a memory. A dream. A dream of dying."[27] He walks throughout the facility and slowly the memory of what was done to him and what he had done begins to return.

He remembers and says, "I am...Logan! I am a man! Animaaal! Animaaal! And you—are the animal! They found me... found me out. Brought me here! Cut me! Got into my body. Tortured me! Tore up my mind! I gotta get away! Gotta get away!"[28]

In many ways, this is what it feels like to enter the Emergency Stage. When you no longer dissociate, you are forced to remember what has happened to you. You may feel as though the only option is to run away. It is like waking up from a nightmare that was real. When this happens, you may feel like your body no longer belongs to you. Your thoughts, actions, and movements may seem foreign because you may have been dissociated from your body for such a long period of time. When you can no longer deny the abuse you suffered, and your feelings come rushing back, you may feel like Logan as he ran to escape the facility saying,

> "I'm runnin'! Runnin' in a dream! I got sticks for legs an' my feet are putty! An' something's behind me. Movin' with me! Like a livin' shadow—it's at my heels... and if I slow down it'll get me—I'll suffocate in it—in its darkness! An' I won't be able to scream...or yell...or fight it off. 'Cos it'll be inside me! Under my skin—in my guts—inside my bones!"[29]

---

27. James, Furwen, and Campanelia, *Marvel Comics Presents Weapon X #84,*
28. James, Furwen, and Campanelia,
29. James, Furwen, and Campanelia,

Unfortunately, you cannot run forever. Feelings and emotions can be repressed, but only for so long. However, eventually those feelings of isolation, loneliness, hatred, and fear rise to the surface. When that happens, those repressed emotions and dissociated memories either negatively impact others, causing them to see you as a villain, or the emotions focus inward, causing you to hate yourself and view yourself as a villain. This means there is only one option for recovery, and that is to face the past, and make the decision to heal. While making this decision is difficult, it allows the flow of emotions, not only negative, but positive too, allowing you to become more intimate with those closest to you. When this occurs, you are able to drop the façade you carry and become the complete individual you were meant to be.

It is an unfortunate fact that bad things happen to good people just as tragedy seems to follow Logan no matter where he goes. However, before passing away, Logan does eventually reconcile his past, confront his abusers, and gain peace over his mind and body. Recovery and healing are the goal. If you do not attempt to reach them, dissociation has the potential to erase memories and create villains as you'll see from Vermin in the next chapter.

CHAPTER SIX

Denial, Believing It Happened, and What It Means to Be a Good Man

Throughout *The Spectacular Spider-Man #178-184* "The Child Within," Dr. Kafka, a female psychologist specializing in trauma abuse and repressed memories, psychoanalyzes a man who resembles and, in many ways, behaves like a rat. Throughout the series, video footage of Dr. Kafka's sessions with the creature who calls himself Vermin depicts a creature whose personality swings on a dime as quickly as a pendulum.

In one image, Vermin cowers in a corner afraid to move, while in the next, he lashes out at Dr. Kafka, willing to kill her without hesitation. In a few images, Vermin even rests his head on Dr. Kafka's arms for comfort. These scenes and their vile portrayal of the human rat makes readers wonder why this ugly "thing" exists in the Spider-Verse. Then Vermin escapes Dr. Kafka's research laboratories and flees into the sewers of New York City where, out of thin air, a pudgy eight-year-old black boy with stiff hair, shorts, and a short-sleeved black-and-white striped shirt appears. The boy asks Vermin to take him home, and that's when the character's story arc takes an interesting and confusing turn.

In the beginning, Vermin is confused. He lashes out, believing the boy has the potential to be his next meal. However, throughout the characters' interaction, the boy's expression never changes. He never screams, and he remains calm as he tells Vermin he is afraid and wants to go home. Uncertain why, Vermin exits the sewer with the boy in his arms to take him home.

It is night when the two arrive at the gate of a large mansion. Inside, asleep, is an elderly married couple comprised of a black woman and white man. Outside the gate, Vermin tells the boy he knows this place and enters the mansion alone. When he enters, he lays down in bed beside the elderly man and calls him father. Confused and afraid, the elderly man shoots Vermin in the shoulder as he flees into the night.

As the story continues, readers come to understand that Vermin's real name is Edward, and that the little black boy is a result of Vermin's suppression of his inner child and denial of childhood sexual abuse at the hands of his father. Throughout these first few comics of "The Child Within," Vermin behaves as if he is remembering the details of a nightmare. He feels that he knows the boy he is taking home, but he cannot remember his name. He believes the man lying asleep in bed is his father, but how? This chapter explores why male survivors often **deny** their childhood sexual abuse happened, and live behind the **façade** of what they believe it means to be a "real" man.

Understanding Denial and Living Behind a Façade

As a male survivor, you have learned to cope, rather than heal, from the abuse you've suffered as a child. Coping may have meant working to the point of no longer acknowledging the trauma you suffered, becoming a perfectionist, or overachieving in school, sports, and work. One of the major coping strategies you may have utilized as a child, and now as an adult, is **denial** that you were ever sexually abused. It may also involve denying that the sexual abuse you suffered as a child has affected your relationship with members of your family, interactions with your partners, or your inability to follow through with goals you have set for yourself professionally and personally. Denial can cause you to blame others for the problems that have arisen in your life, whether that blame is aimed at your abuser, friends, family, loved ones, coworkers, or any other person who challenges your thoughts and beliefs. Continued denial of the abuse you suffered can become an infection that seeps into all parts of your life. If left untreated, it can cause you to no longer consider yourself a survivor and to react and interact with others in the manner of a victim—someone who is only capable of being constantly abused and mistreated throughout all aspects of their life. Possible reasons for this denial may be to:

- protect yourself from remembering traumatic events of the past
- help yourself cope with the fact that you were once a child with no power to protect yourself from abuse
- allow you the ability to conserve energy needed to work and survive
- allow you to prevent hurting yourself or others

Judith Herman explains in her book *Trauma and Recov-*

ery that to survive, children develop the ability to *doublethink* while also creating a *double-self* in an attempt to remain safe and make sense of their hostile environment. This is like hiding behind a mask or a **façade.** Double thinking means having the ability to create and keep positive thoughts and memories alongside those of utter despair. Doing this preserves the possibility of hope and the chance of a possible savior.

For male survivors, double thinking often looks like this: you know you were sexually abused as a child, but you also perpetuate the belief that men and boys cannot be sexually abused or raped. The ability to doublethink walls off the abuse to help you minimize its effects, rationalize why it occurred, or excuse it altogether. It allows the survivor to function, make sense of their abuse, and remain sane while navigating a hostile environment.

Double thinking also creates double self-images for the survivor, fragmenting their identity. On one side, survivors may view themselves and their actions as being "tainted" or "bad." They believe their past abuse gives them the strength to save others. This is because some male survivors believe they are beyond redemption, able to endure what others cannot. These are the thoughts of male survivors who view themselves and their actions as heroes. Other survivors view themselves and their past actions as irredeemable, causing them to believe they are beyond salvation. These are the survivors who view themselves and their actions as those of a villain.

Both the hero and villain mindsets are fragmented and flawed because they force the survivor to view his surroundings through the black-and-white lens of a comic book that cannot be maintained into adulthood. While effective as children, double-thoughts and double-selves do not work when trying to navigate adult relationships. Soon, usually in their late twenties or early to mid-thirties, male survivors realize their world is not a comic book, and the black-and-white images of superheroes and villains shatter. The coping mechanisms once used to survive, thrive, and make sense of oneself, others, one's actions, and one's environment, become less effective. When the denial of their childhood trauma becomes impossible, the reality that men and boys can be sexually assaulted settles in. Then, the abuse becomes more apparent.

Unfortunately, when this breakdown of a male survivor's reality begins to occur, many men refuse to seek help to healthfully address their childhood trauma and heal. Often, men believe mental illness and trauma are not medical conditions, but moral decisions. This comes from societal expectations that "real" men should be capable of remaining emotionally distant, and this stereotype prevents men from doing what is necessary to stay in touch with their emotions and remain capable of nurturing relationships.

Real Men Don't...

Unfortunately, society teaches men (in the same way it teaches women), what it means to be a "real man." These ideas are perpetuated through the words individuals use and the images we see in movies, shows, magazines, and comics. Men, like women, are told from the moment of birth what is socially acceptable. This starts with babies being placed in either blue or pink hats and socks, and the tells continue both verbally and nonverbally. As both genders mature, hints of what is and is not acceptable are sprinkled into countless interactions. These ideas are reiterated by parents, relatives, teachers, and other children. Words of praise and/or shame, such as "my little princess," "you're my big man," "cute," "handsome," "you throw like a girl," "don't be a pussy," "fag," and "man up," all retain these preexisting ideas.

Stigmas of what it means to be a "real" man begin when men are boys. William S. Pollack explains in his book *Real Boys: Rescuing Our Sons from the Myths of Boyhood* that boys are socialized into following the "boy code." This code involves four simple but devastating rules.

1. **The sturdy oak:** Men should be stoic, independent, and refrain from showing weakness.
2. **Give 'em hell:** Boys and men should be macho, take risks, and use violence.
3. **The big wheel:** Men should demonstrate their power and dominance and how they've got everything under control, even if they don't.
4. **No sissy stuff:** Real men don't cry or display emotions that might be viewed as feminine; doing so leaves men open to being labeled as "sissies" or "fags."[30]

It is because of this code that Michael Kimmel says in his article for *New York Magazine* that you should "Raise Your Son to be a Good Man, not a 'Real' Man." When asked what defined a "real" man, boys stated that a "real" man:

- never cries
- is strong
- doesn't show his feelings
- plays through the pain

---

30. Pollack, *Real Boys: Rescuing our Sons from the Myths of Boyhood*.

- sucks it up
- has power
- shows aggression/is aggressive
- wins at all costs
- gets rich
- and gets laid

However, when these same boys were asked what it meant to be a good man, they responded that a good man:

- has integrity
- has honor
- is responsible
- is a good provider
- is a protector
- does the right thing
- puts others first
- makes sacrifice
- is caring
- and stands up for the little guy[31]

Unfortunately, this perpetuated belief that males need to be "real" men rather than good men has taught boys to hold in their emotions and not show signs of affection. Instead, boys believe they should remain dominant, sure, and confident at all times. To do anything else would risk being viewed as less than a "real" man. It is for this reason that when a traumatic event such as childhood sexual abuse occurs, males have no way of managing the emotions they are feeling. Thus, they dissociate and deny the abuse ever occurred. This often leads to feelings

---

31. Kimmel.

of overwhelming anger and powerlessness, which many men express as dominance. Sometimes, rather than outward expressions of anger and isolation, perpetuated beliefs of toxic masculinity such as stoicism, violence, and promiscuity can lead to internal vehemence and self-destruction. This can cause male survivors to feel so alone and isolated that they believe their only option is suicide. In fact, men die by suicide 3.53 times more often than women, according to the American Foundation for Suicide Prevention.

Vermin can help you understand the impact of living behind a façade. He demonstrates what happens when someone tries to live up to societal standards of a "real" man and what occurs when their double-thoughts begin to crumble.

Vermin and Believing the Abuse Happened

As the six-part saga of "The Child Within" continues, Vermin reveals his true identity through a series of conversations with himself and Dr. Kafka. Vermin says to Dr. Kafka, "No, don't make me tell. It always hurts so much when I tell."[32]

"It hurts when you don't tell, Edward. Telling heals you," she responds. Vermin then reveals the nature of his sexual abuse. He says,

> "The Judge. The Judge comes into my bedroom. I can't even sleep anymore. I just lay there...waiting for him to come. He looks like my father—but—he can't be! My father wouldn't do...wouldn't do the bad thing! He–he touches me! And he makes me touch

---

32. DeMatteis, Buscema, *The Spectacular Spider-Man* #

him! And it makes me feel so bad...Makes me sick and sorry at the same time! Can't think about it! Can't let myself remember! Gotta push it away! Push it way down deep. Into the sewers. Edward's gone. I'm Vermin!!"

This excerpt helps to understand how Vermin was created. Edward Whelan's repressed memories and emotions about the sexual abuse committed by his father caused Edward to create the other identity, one that reflects the creature he believes himself to be: a vermin.

Edward's words and feelings likely feel familiar when he states, "Can't think about it! Can't let myself remember! Gotta push it away! Push it way down deep." Rather than remember the horrific abuses, Edward copes in the same manner as so many survivors of childhood sexual abuse. He pushes the memory of the trauma so far down that he represses all other emotions as well, leaving himself emotionally stunted and able to only express anger or confusion. Rather than place the blame on the perpetrator, Edward blames himself for not being able to stop the abuse.

As a male survivor, you may also feel as if you are a vermin, disgusting, and unable to be loved. You may also blame yourself for the abuse you endured. Society has perpetuated the belief that men and boys cannot be raped or abused. Because of this belief, many males have internalized the abuse they endured as children as being their fault. They've internalized the pain and repressed their emotions. Vermin also states, "There must have been some way I could have stopped it. Why didn't I stop it? I feel so guilty, like a criminal. Worse than a criminal. Ugly. Vile. Beyond redemption. An animal. Obscene. Inhuman.

Vermin."[33]

In this passage Edward reveals feelings of self-hatred after he has begun his journey of healing. Many survivors feel similarly toward themselves after being sexually abused. Like Vermin, survivors feel as if they are disgusting and less than human. They feel vile and unworthy of love. Rather than remember being a good, wholesome boy who endured pain when he was sexually abused, Edward is pushed away and replaced by a disgusting creature no one wants. He believes himself to be like garbage left in the sewers. To survive, Edward dissociates from his body and creates Vermin to protect himself from experiencing further abuse. Unfortunately, memories and emotions cannot be repressed forever. They must rise to the surface eventually. Edward proves this when he states,

"Everyone lies! Everyone hides behind a mask! Thought they could keep me locked up...hidden away...behind the walls...behind the masks, but I showed them. Can't keep me locked away. Don't tell anybody! Go down into the dark. Into the sewers—like a worthless little rat! Hide it away! Hide it away! Well, I'm not hiding anymore!"[34]

Although suppressing the memory of your sexual abuse may have once been the only way to survive, the memories of the sexual abuse must be addressed if healing is going to take place. The mask you wear must come off to reveal the person behind the façade. Hiding the pain away and not addressing the abuse only leads to more pain. The sexual abuse you en-

33. DeMatteis, Buscema,
34. DeMatteis, Buscema,

dured was not your fault. There is nothing you could have done to prevent the abuse from occurring. Accepting this statement as fact and moving beyond feelings of self-hatred takes time. It takes not only knowing, but accepting that it was not your fault.

The story ends with Vermin returning to his childhood home. Rather than cuddling with his father as he did before, he returns angry. Teeth drawn and filled with rage, Vermin enters the room of his father, gripping the hair of his mother as she cowers on the ground. Vermin confronts his father but is unable to go through with killing the man. Afterward, he is comforted by his mother. She says she will protect him. Hearing this, Vermin becomes angry again, but this time toward his mother. He demands to know why she did not protect him when his father was touching and hurting him. Unfortunately, Vermin states that he is no longer Edward. Edward is gone. There is only Vermin.

In the same way Wolverine's mother, Elizabeth Howlett, called her son an animal when she saw what he had become, Vermin's parents no longer see him as their son. In fact, both Wolverine and Vermin battle feelings of being more animal than man. They no longer see themselves as men. You may battle with your own manhood as you begin to remember and reconcile your childhood sexual abuse. In this stage of the healing process, you must accomplish the difficult task of acknowledging that the abuse did happen. It is the only way to move forward. Edward demonstrates this can be done in the final appearance of Vermin in *The Spectacular Spider-Man* *#185*. In this issue, Dr. Kafka suppresses the appearance of Vermin and brings Edward back, but only for a short time. Soon, Vermin rises to the surface, pushing Edward down, and fighting for his own survival as a personality created to protect

Edward. Dr. Kafka explains that, "All these years, a part of Edward, the deepest part, has believed he deserved to be trapped in that hideous form."[35]

When you begin to heal, there will no longer be a need to cope with your sexual abuse by forgetting, dissociating, or presenting a façade. The masks and identity you created to survive will associate into one consciousness called the Self, creating the complete person you were meant to be. However, **association** is not simple. Many coping mechanisms may have been a part of your life for years, making them difficult, but not impossible, to put away.

---

35. DeMatteis, Buscema,

CHAPTER SEVEN

Kraven the Hunter, Self-Harm, and Understanding the Perpetration of Childhood Sexual Abuse

If there is any character in the Marvel or DC universe that embodies the definition of being a "real" man, it is Kraven the Hunter. With jet-black slicked-back hair; an open, sleeveless lion's pelt as a vest; broad shoulders, bulging biceps, rippling pectorals, and six-pack abs, Kraven prides himself as being the best hunter—man or beast—to walk the face of the Earth.

Kraven makes his first appearance in *The Amazing Spider-Man #15*, "Kraven the Hunter." His true name is Sergei Kravinoff. His parents were Russian nobility, and throughout his existence in the Spider-Verse, the villain has used his wealth and aristocracy to travel the world, hunting the most dangerous animals to become the world's greatest hunter. However, unlike other big-game hunters, Kraven does not use guns or modern weapons. Instead, the villain hunts using his bare hands, and traps and weapons he creates in the wild. He also has a secret magical serum that gives him super strength. This villain is unique because he hunts by a code of honor, choosing only to battle his prey fairly.

Although Kraven's abilities, physique, and wealth make him everything society would deem a "real" man, the character still views himself as less of a man than Spider-Man. This assessment causes him to commit suicide in "Kraven's Last Hunt." Understanding why Kraven took his life will help you to understand how childhood sexual abuse affects the feelings and thoughts of male survivors, and why it often makes them believe suicide is their only option to escape from their childhood trauma.

Effects of Sexual Abuse on Feelings

As a male survivor of childhood sexual abuse, you may find it difficult to express your emotions. This may be because of a belief that your feelings are dangerous. Coming of age during, and/or after, experiencing a horrific trauma in which your body was violated, may cause you to believe you cannot afford to feel the full range of your terror, pain, shame, or rage, because the results would be too catastrophic if those pent-up emotions were to explode out at those you care for. You may also believe that because you were sexually abused, your body is no longer safe. Unfortunately, this may mean isolating your emotions and feelings as if a stranger inhabits your body. According to *The Courage to Heal*, surviving childhood sexual abuse may make it difficult to [36]:

---

36. Bass, Davis,

- recognize your feelings
- differentiate between emotions
- express feelings
- calm down when you get upset

As a survivor, you may also feel:

- disconnected, isolated, and alone
- a pervasive sense of shame
- just a few feelings, rather than a full range of emotions
- out of control with your rage or feelings
- dead inside

You, as a survivor, may have a pervasive sense of shame because of your perceived sense of weakness stemming from your inability to prevent your sexual abuse. You may feel pleasure remotely, and rarely, if ever, be capable of relaxing and enjoying life. Instead of feeling shame and viewing yourself as less of a man for being unable to capture Spider-Man (like Kraven), you may have a sense of shame when facing the undeniable truth that you had no way of preventing your sexual abuse. The pleasure and joy you feel in life may be minimal, much like Kraven's limited emotions when he is consumed with what it means to be a "real" man in "Kraven's Last Hunt."

Kraven the Hunter and Suicide

"Kraven's Last Hunt" is a five-part epic graphic novel that spans three different comic series: *Web of Spider-Man #31* "Part One: The Coffin," *Web of Spider-Man #32* "Part Four: Resurrection," *The Amazing Spider-Man #293* "Part Two:

Crawling," *The Amazing Spider-Man #294* "Part Five: Thunder," *Peter Parker the Spectacular Spider-Man #131* "Part Three: Descent," and *Peter Parker the Spectacular Spider-Man #132* "Part Six: Ascending." On the first pages of the comic, Kraven sets the tone for manliness when he battles a wild bear while naked and knocks its head off with his bare hands. Afterward, he climbs the stairs to his mansion, puts on a silk robe, and drinks a glass of wine. I can think of nothing more "manly" or suave.

Although Kraven seems to be a man's man, he believes and feels at his core that he is nothing. He feels this way because no matter how hard he has tried in the past, he has not been able to defeat Spider-Man. He prides himself on being the best hunter in the world, but the sleek, thin, nimble, agile, nerdy, bookworm who prides himself on being "friendly" has bested him at every turn. If Kraven is viewed by society as being everything a "real" man should be, then Spider-Man is his antithesis. To be repeatedly defeated by a "lesser" man is more than Kraven can endure. Kraven believes he is living a lie, so in "Kraven's Last Hunt," though he has grown older, and his health is beginning to decline, he makes one final attempt to defeat Spider-Man and prove he is the better hunter and a "real" man.

To seek his revenge, Kraven captures Spider-Man and buries him in a coffin for two-weeks. During that time, Kraven assumes Spider-Man's identity, wears his costume, and fights crime as a bloodthirsty vigilante. When Spider-Man rises from the grave to hunt down Kraven for what he has done, Spider-Man discovers the villain no longer wishes to fight. In fact, he seems happy to surrender. He explains to Spider-Man how he has become a better hero than Spider-Man could ever be. The web-slinger senses no danger from Kraven, so he leaves.

Soon after Spider-Man departs, Kraven places a shotgun in his mouth, pulls the trigger, and kills himself.

Understanding why Kraven committed suicide can help you understand why male survivors may feel that suicide is their only option when faced with the reality of their childhood trauma. First, it is important to understand the difference between a survivor, victim, and perpetrator (of which Kraven is the latter). He is not a hero, no matter what he may have done while pretending to be one. This is because abuse is all about power.

Following the victimization of childhood sexual abuse, an individual loses control over their life. The perpetrator strips the victim of their sense of safety. Perpetrators of sexual abuse victimize others to regain a sense of control over their life. They do this by taking the power and safety of another. Their desire to feel that they can control the outcomes of their own life lead them to abuse others. This is precisely what Kraven does when he locks Spider-Man in a coffin and assumes his identity for two weeks.

After losing battle after battle with Spider-Man, Kraven attempted to regain his sense of control by hijacking the life of the web-crawler. This action sealed the hunter's fate as a villain and perpetrator, no matter what good deeds he may have done while wearing Spider-Man's costume.

Following Spider-Man's escape, Kraven made the choice to commit suicide partially because he succeeded in stealing Spider-Man's power, and partially because he believed he would no longer qualify as a "real" man when he aged and his mystical serum became less effective. Kraven's toxic beliefs in what it means to be a "real" man meant he could not find value in his strength, wealth, or abilities as a hunter unless he was the best and could remain the best. He looked toward the future, saw a list of failures, and believed his only option was suicide. As a male survivor, you may have the same form of absolute thinking due to the trauma you suffered as a child. Without healing and recovery, you may only be able to see your short-comings and inabilities to live up to the false expectations of what it means to be a "real" man. This form of thinking is dangerous. It makes you believe, as Kraven did, that suicide is preferable to risking failure.

Another possible reason Kraven committed suicide (and why you as a male survivor may contemplate taking your own life), is that after reaching his goal, Kraven believed he had nothing left to live for. As a villain, Kraven spent his days at-tempting to regain his honor as the world's greatest hunter and prove that he was better than Spider-Man. This became his life purpose. When he successfully bested Spider-Man, regained his honor, and became the world's best hunter, he had nothing left to strive for in his life. According to the book *Happier*, by Tal Ben-Shahar, Ph.D, this is called the *arrival fallacy*. Ben-Sha-har explains how this is the "false belief that reaching a valued destination can sustain happiness."[37] Kraven suffers from this fallacy and grapples with the meaning of his life after achiev-ing his goal to be the best hunter in the world.

From Kraven's perspective, he could only fall from grace as his health continued to deteriorate and old age became a real-ity. He had no wife, son, daughter, or apprentice to train and pass his skills on to. He was staring at a seemingly impossible void to fill. As a male survivor, you may be similar to Kraven in the goals you seek throughout your life. Living to fulfill false expectations of an ideal male image of the perfect body, car, job, or gadget while refusing to be fully intimate with the peo-

---

37. Ben-Shahar, *Happier*.

ple you care for creates a hollow life. This hollowness will never be able to be filled by stuff. Until you seek recovery and healing from your past childhood sexual abuse, you will never feel complete. You may start to think your only option to stop feeling so alone is to end the pain through suicide. Like Kraven, one day you may reach your goal and have every material possession you wish for. When this happens, and you have not taken the time to care for yourself and share a life with those closest to you, you will feel more alone than ever. Like Kraven, you'll have reached the top and your only option will be to fall. The toxic thoughts Kraven demonstrates about what it means to be a "real" man help to explain why men are 3.5 times more likely to commit suicide than women according to the American Foundation for Suicide Prevention. Know that suicide should never be an option. The goal of this part of the book is to help you learn to change your automatic thoughts and cognitive distortions so you'll no longer think in the absolute terms that can lead to suicide. Healing from your past trauma and filling the void left after being sexually abused will offer a better understanding of yourself and the strength you have as a survivor.

One sexual abuse is not greater or less than another. It only takes one occurrence of sexual abuse to be a survivor, no matter how small that occurence may seem. The primary reason is that while the effects of sexual abuse may not be visible on the surface, the abuse will have lasting negative effects. Just as each sexual abuse is not greater or less severe than another, each lead to different expressions of the same effects of loneliness, isolation, loss of identity, disgrace, pain, fear, and limited expression of emotions. Like all the other coping mechanisms, self-harm is an attempt to relieve those effects and feel normal, loved, wanted, and alive.

Although self-harm is severe and can lead to death, like treating wounds, you can heal from the sexual abuse of your childhood. As a male survivor of childhood sexual abuse, no matter what you may have endured or been told, you did not deserve to be abused. You did nothing wrong. You are a good person. You do have self-worth. You make a difference. Fight to remind yourself of this fact every day you open your eyes and breathe another breath. You are a human being deserving of healing. The next chapter will help you understand and transform your cognitive distortions. It will also recognize the life you could have lived if you had never been sexually abused.

CHAPTER EIGHT

Remembering and Child, Parent, Adult (CPA) Thoughts

During and after the Emergency Stage, memories of childhood sexual abuse may fade and return in the same way memories of being James Howlett ebbed and flowed for Wolverine as he pieced together his past. These memories are different from those acquired during day-to-day interactions. Nonthreatening memories, such as what was eaten for dinner or the finite details of all eighteen movies leading up to *Avengers: Infinity War*, can be recollected without serious strain. However, memories of sexual abuse have similar, if not the same effects, on the mind and body as other traumatic events like mass shootings, bombings, natural disasters, and hostage situations. Such situations affect not only the mind, but the body. *The Body Keeps the Score* explains how:

> Trauma affects the entire human organism—body, mind, and brain. In PTSD the body continues to defend against a threat that belongs to the past. Healing from

PTSD means being able to terminate this continued stress mobilization and restore the entire organism to safety. After trauma the world is experienced with a different nervous system. The survivor's energy now becomes focused on suppressing inner chaos, at the expense of spontaneous involvement in their life. These attempts to maintain control over unbearable physiological reactions can result in a whole range of physical symptoms, including fibromyalgia, chronic fatigue, and other autoimmune diseases. This explains why it is critical for trauma treatment to engage the entire organism, body, mind, and brain.[38]

Peter Parker, Remembering, and Changing Childlike Thoughts

Peter Parker has suffered a traumatic past in many of the same ways as Wolverine. Peter lost his surrogate father, Uncle Ben, and both of his birthparents as a child. Like Wolverine, he saw his first romantic love murdered before his eyes. These painful memories make it difficult for Peter to recall his past. However, when these memories come rushing back after years of repression, Peter seeks the help of psychologist Dr. Kafka to cope with the memories of his past and view himself as an adult rather than a child.

Throughout "The Child Within" saga, there are references to the grave and dying. This allusion to death and the grave began six comics prior when Peter was buried alive by Kraven for two weeks while the villain assumed his identity as Spi-

---

38. Kolk, van der, *The Body Keeps the Score*.

der-Man. (Again, this is a comic book, so suspend a little disbelief.) The trauma of losing two weeks of his life haunts the hero while he visits the grave of his dead parents.

While visiting his parents' grave, Peter reflects on his past, how he hardly remembers them, and how now, after being dead for so many years, they are now practically strangers to him. However, later in the saga, after Peter is drugged by Harry Osbourn, his memories of his parents resurface.

After being drugged by Harry, Peter begins to hallucinate. The drugs transport the hero to a cemetery surrounded by the graves of people who have died in Peter's life. Throughout the scene, Peter says things that indicate the burden of guilt he carries for living while others he loved died. For example, he blames himself for Uncle Ben's death since he did not stop the killer when he had the chance. As the hallucinations continue, Peter reveals the guilt he feels for his parent's death.

In his final hallucinations, Peter has a complete breakdown. He remembers and relives the death of his parents as if he were a child. The fear, anger, and blame rush to the surface, causing him to burst into a fit of rage. The emotions expressed on his face show uncontrollable panic and provide a great scene of how it feels to become immersed in the Emergency Stage of healing. Peter has no control over the flood of emotions that come over him. Likewise, as a survivor, your emotions may feel out of control when you are triggered to recall the sexual abuse you suffered.

However, what is stark about these comics is the language Peter uses to describe how he feels toward the loss of his parents. As he suffers the hallucination and relives the memory of learning that his parents had died, Peter says, "Please lord they can't be dead! Don't let them be dead! I'll do anything! I'll be good I swear! Don't let them be dead! DON'T LET THEM BE

DEAD!! Daddy Mommy Mommy Daddy Mommy Daddy went away! They must not love me! It must be my fault they went away! It must be my fault!"

Peter says these words while wildly swinging through New York City without his mask. The traumatic event of being buried alive by Kraven caused Peter to suffer the flood of memories. Afterward, dominoes begin to fall, and a cascade of memories and emotions Peter believed he had healed from and stored away resurface. Peter's tone and use of childlike language is an example of how memories can come rushing back, causing the survivor to enter the Emergency Stage. Triggers that lead to the Emergency Stage do not have to be as dramatic as being buried alive, but they could be anything that cause the dominoes of mental blocks to fall away, revealing the nature of the childhood trauma. As discussed previously, the trigger could be as simple as a smell, the mention of a news article, or a scene from a movie, or it could be as complex as the birth of a child or death of a family member. The trick is to associate these memories so you can know the trauma did occur, but not be extremely affected by the memory.

Later in the comic, as Dr. Kafka speaks and attempts to pull Peter's consciousness back from the brink, he arises from a dark abyss.

In these scenes, Peter's use of language is important. His voice and tone sound like that of a little boy. He says, "But I feel like a little boy. Justa bad, bad little boy." He no longer speaks as an adult. He sounds powerless because that is how he feels. You may find, as a male survivor of childhood sexual abuse, that when you recall or speak about the sexual abuse you endured as a child, your voice becomes that of your child-self because in the same way Peter feels helpless while remembering his past trauma, you may feel this way as well. No matter how much power you have accumulated as an adult, without making the decision to heal you will always feel like that weak boy who is not worthy of being loved. In 1986, James Pennebaker at the University of Texas in Austin confirms this theory when he discovered that when an individual talked about a traumatic event from their past, their voice changed in tone and style. Not only that, but their handwriting changed, as did their facial expressions and body movements. Pennebaker's study found that when an individual who has suffered a traumatic event expresses the reality of the traumatic event, their handwriting, voice, and movements "switch" to become more childlike and primitive. Peter demonstrates this "switch" from adult to childlike thoughts when he says, for example, "They went away because they don't love me," or "It's my fault."

However, when Dr. Kafka tells Peter, "You can be a little boy and spend the rest of your life afraid and guilty. You can wrap that guilt around yourself and hide in it forever—or you can tuck that little boy away in your heart. Be a father to him," Peter's tone begins to shift. He tells himself he is a man, making the decision to heal from his childhood trauma to regain the strength that was stripped away. As a male survivor, making the choice to forgive the child you have locked away will provide you with the same strength needed to begin viewing yourself as a good man deserving of love.

Peter behaves, thinks, and acts as if he were a child. As a male survivor of childhood sexual abuse, you may experience moments of panic and anxiety in the same manner as Peter. When entering the Emergency Stage, memories of the past come flooding back. In that moment, you may believe or say it was your fault. You may also believe that you were a "bad boy." You may feel as though you are a helpless child, unable to defend yourself from the abuse you suffered. However, you must remember the memory of the past can no longer hurt you. In the same way Peter states, "I am a man!" you must know and believe that now you are also a man.

Make the decision to heal and become a good man of intelligence and worth. Throughout the rest of this chapter, you will work to heal, remember, and forgive the little boy who was sexually abused, and to accept the fact that you did nothing wrong to deserve that abuse.

Writing Exercise #5: Child, Parent, Adult (CPA) Thoughts

The child who was sexually abused is hidden and locked away. To survive and become what the male believed to be a "real" man, he may have had to lock that child away. This meant the need to have emotions and trust in others the way other children did also got locked away. Because of childhood sexual abuse, it can be difficult for a survivor to even remember being a child. Portions of their childhood may be a blank slate, creating a sense that they were never a child, or that they have always been the stoic male who seemed to carry the weight of the world on his shoulders. This is true.

The falsehood of that belief may not become fully unearthed until the birth of a child, or the time when that child reaches the age in which the survivor was sexually abused. When this happens, the survivor may find himself becoming a villain rather than a hero as he experiences unpredictable moments of rage and anxiety, such as when Harry Osbourn fought to maintain his denial of his childhood abuse by his father, Norman Osbourn. The only cure is to make contact with the little boy inside, and to make peace with him in the same way that Peter made peace with his inner child.

Male survivors may find themselves saying to their inner child, "Stop being so weak," "You can push harder than that," and "You still have more you can give and do if you stop holding back!" These statements are abusive to the inner child and continue the mindset of having little-to-no self-worth. Altering the cognitive distortions and reframing automatic thoughts to those of an adult will create better mental health and long-term, lasting happiness.

Altering these thoughts cannot be accomplished overnight, but the abuse of the inner child must be recognized. When harsh words are being directed at the inner child, change the words to those of praise and encouragement. Make peace in the knowledge that the inner child is doing his very best, and nothing more can be asked of him. When you reach this understanding, you will no longer view your inner child as the bad guy, but as a person deserving of love and support the same as anyone else. Then, you will truly know the sexual abuse was in no way your fault. You did not have the strength to stop it then, but you are strong now.

A simple strategy to help change distorted automatic thoughts can be to label and change the thoughts from the type belonging to a child or demanding parent, to those of a supportive adult.

- **Childish Thoughts:** These thoughts are filled with excuses and blame. For example, Harry said to Peter during his hallucination, "Peter—I'm sorry—but you made me do this. You understand that don't you? Every time I find a little peace inside myself, every time I start to believe...really believe...that my father was a good man—I see your face in

front of me—listing all of Norman Osbourn's crimes."
Rather than explore his or his father's role in the problem,
he blames Peter. Your thoughts may behave the same way.
Rather than explore your role in the possible problem, you
feel your actions are justified and looked down on by others, when they should be praised.

- **Parental Thoughts:** These thoughts are filled with
  "should" and "must" statements, making the survivor
  believe they have no choice. For example, when Peter
  was hallucinating, he says, "They must not love me! It
  must be my fault they went away! It must be my fault!"
  Although Peter is behaving like a child, his voice is similar to that of an adult chastising a child. He blames himself for his parent's death when he had no control over
  the situation in the same way you, as a male survivor,
  blame yourself even though you had no control over
  your sexual abuse. You may find that your thoughts and
  words are akin to Peter's. Rather than acknowledging
  the limitations of your actions and speaking positive
  words of encouragement to yourself, you are instead
  stating what you "must" do, or "should" have done.

- **Adult Thoughts:** The goal of this exercise is to reframe
  the automatic thoughts so that they are no longer those
  of an uncompromising parent, or a child controlled by
  denial, needs, and wants. For example, Dr. Kafka says to
  Peter, "You've faced the monster. You've looked it square
  in the eye. It can't hurt you anymore." Dr. Kafka acknowledges Peter's accomplishment in facing his past
  and beginning his journey to become a complete individual. She helps and guides Peter to change his automatic
  thoughts to resemble those of an adult. This takes practice and help from a counselor or therapist, so you'll

want to find your own Dr. Kafka.

In this writing exercise, work with your therapist, counselor, or support system to identify the automatic thoughts that are those of a child or parent, and think of how to reframe them into those of an adult. To help with this process, use the graphic organizer below.

Automatic Thought Exercise				
Automatic Thought	Childish Reasoning	Parental Reasoning	Adult Reasoning	Changed Automatic Thoughts
Peter—I'm sorry—but you made me do this. You understand that don't you? Every time I find a little peace inside myself, every time I start to believe…really believe…that my father was a good man—I see your face in front of me—listing all of Norman Osbourn's crimes.	X			Everyone is in control of his or her own actions.
They must not love me! It must be my fault they went away! It must be my fault!		X		Their death had nothing to do with how much they loved me.
You've faced the monster. You've looked it square in the eye. It can't hurt you anymore.			X	The past cannot hurt me anymore.

Remembering

Remembering the nature of your sexual abuse is difficult. Knowing you were sexually abused and remembering you were sexually abused is difficult. Pieces of the abuse may come out at separate times, and rather than memories, you may experience physical sensations. Piecing these memories together will help you understand and accept that men and boys can be the victim of childhood sexual abuse. Writing the memories in a journal throughout the Emergency Stage can help you to verify your emotions and reassert the reality that this did happen to you. However, if at any time the memories become too overwhelming, stop. Visit your safe place. And do not continue the exercise until you feel comfortable. Discuss these memories, emotions, and your writing with your counselor or therapist. Do not continue if they advise you to stop.

Writing Exercise #6: Journaling to Remember

Remembering is difficult and may seem impossible. Entire portions of your life may appear empty and incomplete. To assist in remembering, it may be helpful to:

- **Look at pictures from your childhood.** If available go through family photo albums or images saved on social media websites.
- **Look up what movies were in theatres or what major events were happening in the news during the period you cannot remember.** Sometimes the only way to remember what was happening in your life is by remembering what was happening in the world. If comfortable,

watch, read, or listen to your favorites from the past.

- **Look at old yearbooks.** Attempt to remember who your friends, enemies, and teachers were. These were the people you spent much of your time with as a child.

- **Review past report cards.** Remember the kind of student you were. Did you get straight As? Where you a class clown? Read the teacher comments to piece together the person you were.

Below is the story of my sexual abuse as a male survivor. I've included it to help you know you are not alone. This story was originally published in *Raped Black Male: A Memoir.* Please be warned, my story may be triggering. If you are not in a safe place physically, mentally, or emotionally, it may be beneficial to skip this section. Portions of my story can be graphic at times. If you do begin reading any portion of my story and it begins to cause you distress, please stop reading and return when you are ready. There is no shame in knowing your limits. In fact, this is what makes you strong. Be kind to yourself and move with caution along your own journey of healing.

Men Can't Be Raped (Autobiographical)

I wish I had a better memory of what occurred the first time I was raped, but it's been over twenty years and some of the memories have become hazy. I do know the house was empty of my parents and brother. What's interesting is that the first time wasn't the first time. It began with my abuser and a pornographic tape. My abuser was my sister and, at the time, babysitter. I would often have a babysitter when Mom had to work late at K-Mart, or Dad went out and had to DJ at The American Legion. My parents also simply went out sometimes (as parents should), or they didn't get home from work until after 5:00 p.m. when I got out of school and home about 3:15/3:30. So, during that time, when we were alone, is when the grooming began.

Knowing and understanding grooming is not what you may think. It's not when two individuals sit down and brush and comb the other's hair like chimps in a zoo. Grooming is a term used to explain how abusers prepare their victim for molestation. For some abusers, it occurs when their victim runs around, becoming excited while playing tag, for example. Then, instead of the abuser tagging their victim, the abuser grabs the genitals, breasts, or puts their hands down the victim's pants. Anything to get the child sexually aroused and excited while making their victim believe they are safe and participating in a fun game. Afterward, the roles are reversed. The abuser has the victim run, tag, and touch them in the same way. This makes the victim believe this is how the game is played and allows the abuser to open the door to more egregious acts and games where the abuser can easily sexually assault with less resistance and more severity.

My grooming occurred in the form of pornographic movies.

My dad had a collection of pornographic videocassettes under the mattress of the bed in the basement of our home that were easily accessible and could easily be replaced after they were used as if they were never touched. Eventually, after the basement had been remodeled and the bed and mattress were thrown in the trash, the cassettes were moved to the bottom drawer of the desk in the basement.

The reason I remember this bed so vividly is because my

sister, Daniel, and I would often play on the mattress when my parents were gone. Both would have me lay on the mattress while they would run and jump on the bed to try and fling me into the air and against the wall. I loved it. Just crazy, stupid, innocent stuff kids do when their parents are gone—unlike what eventually happened when Daniel moved away after physically fighting with my father.

The grooming began one afternoon when my parents were gone. I was being babysat, and she asked with a calm, happy smile after entering my room, "Hey Kenny, wanna see something cool?" Of course, I agreed. I was eight years old. I lived for cool. Cool was my life, and she knew it.

From my room, she led me down to the basement, lifted the mattress, removed the black cassette tape, and placed it in the VCR. I remember that the cassette wasn't labeled as pornography, instead it had a normal white label on the spine of the cassette, as if it had once been a different movie that had been taped over. Because it looked like so many other movies in our library, I never suspected the contents the movie actually contained.

Like most movies in the 80s and 90s paused in the middle of the cassette, it didn't start at the beginning. Instead, it continued from the last moment my father hit stop, which was in the middle of two people moving, groaning, humping, and fitting pieces of their body into places I had no idea was possible at such an age. Immediately, I was disgusted. At the time, I didn't know what it was, but I knew it was a movie I was not supposed to watch.

My eight-year-old brain flashed back to scenes of Spike Lee's *School Daze* and how my parents told me to cover my eyes during the "dirty parts." Seeing what was happening on the screen, I figured this was most definitely a dirty part I wasn't allowed to watch, so I covered my eyes and waited for the okay that the scene had ended and I could open my eyes to something safe. Instead, she took my hands from my eyes and said, "Watch. It's funny." I tried to cover my eyes during a few scenes that followed that were especially embarrassing, but I was coaxed into watching.

Soon it was over. When it came to an end, she rewound the tape to where it began, put the cassette under the mattress, and went back upstairs to continue the day. Nothing happened. She did not try and touch me, or me to touch her. Rather than grooming me to become sexually aroused through a game that allowed us to explore the other's body, she groomed me to like the idea of sex through the use of movies, which were a primary source of entertainment in our house. Any free moment the family had was spent watching a movie. We all had our classic repeats we could (and did) watch over and over again. My mother loved *Toy Soldiers*, *The Five Heartbeats*, and *The Temptations*. Daniel loved *The Last Dragon*. I loved *The Rocketeer* and *Hook*, and my dad simply loved movies in general. Going to Blockbuster on Friday evenings to search the shelves for a new release or an unwatched classic was always on the agenda. Because movies were such a large part of the lives in my family, my abuser had found an in that made grooming through pornographic movies safe, fun, and a common form of entertainment that my eight-year-old self would never question as not being valid and acceptable.

Of course, I knew not to tell about watching the videos. I was never told not to tell, but I just knew. Technically, nothing had happened, and I had been groomed after years of breaking figurines, rules, and going places when my parents left, that what happened when they were gone was not allowed to be discussed unless we were caught. Then, and only then, was I allowed to sing like a bird. It ensured no one got in trouble. Unfortunately, my abuser never got caught.

For months, this is how it went. My parents would leave, she'd get the tape from under the mattress, we'd watch, put it back, and continue with our day, never saying a word to our parents. The only other person to tell that could have stopped the abuse from happening was Daniel, who was eighteen years old at the time, out of high school and attending Alabama A&M in Huntsville, Alabama. Eventually, Daniel dropped out of college after the first year, joined the military, and moved to Germany to raise a family of his own, making him completely unavailable until my early teens. Although the grooming lasted for many months, it eventually turned to something much more sinister.

As time progressed and the grooming continued, my abuser and I no longer sat on the floor together watching the video in silence, disgust, or mock laughter. Instead, each of us had our own positions in the room, separate from the other. She lay on the bed with a comforter over her body, while I sat on the couch and watched the scenes play out on the screen. After months of watching the cassette in secret on weekends or late nights when our parents were gone, I no longer covered my eyes and looked away in embarrassment. In fact, most times I had become sexually aroused. My therapist tells me it's normal because it's a natural reaction of the body after being stimulated by the brain, but I find it hard to not view myself as a protagonist of the sex and abuse, no matter what she tells me. However, I did not masturbate. Mostly because I had no idea what masturbation was or that it was even possible. I was too young to know. My abuser, on the other hand, being five years my senior, was discovering masturbation beneath the comforter on the mattress ten feet away from where I sat while watching a woman receive pleasure from a man in the same way she sexually stimulated herself.

After being groomed to willingly watch pornography while remaining silent of the molestation, becoming sexually aroused, and her being sexually stimulated through masturbation, all the pieces had fallen into place for me to be raped with little resistance—and that's precisely what occurred.

The first time grooming transgressed to rape: my abuser called me to the bed where she lay with the blanket pulled over her body from where I sat on the couch. I looked at the bed and walked over. She said calmly but with a little hesitation, "Let's try something different. Get on top of me." This is when she pulled back the blanket to reveal she had on no pants or panties.

Immediately, I froze. I had no idea what to say or do. I thought to myself, *Is this okay? Can I say no?* I wanted to say no, but I didn't know how. How could I? She was someone I trusted. I thought I had to do what she said. She was my sister. I believed with all my heart, beyond a shadow of a doubt, she wouldn't do anything to hurt me. It's taken nearly thirty years, therapy, and meditation for this belief to finally change.

In the moment, she noticed my hesitation. Seeing all those thoughts run through my head at once, she knew she couldn't give me an option. With more confidence, invitingly but with more force, she said, "Let's do what they do. Come on," as she worked off my pants.

When the rape happened and she placed me on top of her, I didn't move. I lay there, lifeless, uncomfortable, and cold. She was larger, and there was no way for me to touch the mattress, so I lay hovering in the air on top and inside her body as the pornographic movie continued to play in the background. When I didn't move, she became frustrated and annoyed that I wasn't doing it right. Again, she took control over the situation, grabbed me by the waist and made me move up and down, in and out, as she watched the scenes play out on the screen on the other side of the room. It lasted only a few minutes, but the impact has yet to vanish. She finished and I stopped moving. We both got dressed, she rewound the tape, put it back under the mattress as always, but this time was different. Rather than go upstairs to continue our day, she said what she had never said before: don't tell.

"It's bad," she said, "and we'll get in trouble."

I was too young to argue or know what it meant, so I didn't tell. I remained silent, just as she wanted. For over twenty years I remained quiet, because I didn't want to get in trouble. I thought, it was my fault and I'd be punished. There was nothing I could do if I didn't want Mom, Dad, and Daniel to look at me with the shame and regret I felt. I had done something wrong that no one knew had occurred except her, so the best and only option was to keep quiet, never tell, and keep her secret.

How did this make me feel? In the moment, I felt dirty. I curled up inside myself, waiting for it to stop, and I haven't stopped waiting. I didn't say much. There was no kissing or fondling, just sex. And that's how it went for almost two years. Our parents would leave, pornography would play, I would be raped, and I wouldn't tell. Over time, I began to anticipate when it was going to happen, even look forward to it. My therapist says this is natural. She says it's normal to have been aroused and sexually stimulated. It's something the body does and something I couldn't control, but it still doesn't change what I feel, and that is that it was my fault. That I could have stopped it. That I enjoyed it. That I'm to blame, and that no matter what I do I'm damned, with no amount of forgiveness that can bring me back.

Then, without warning, one day, abruptly, the rapes stopped. After church she told me, almost out of the blue, we couldn't do it anymore because it was wrong and that it never happened. I said okay, but my mind was racing. One thought after the other came without stop. *You did this to me and now you're saying we can't do it anymore? And you're telling me it never happened? You're telling me it was wrong? How wrong was it? Why was it wrong? What's going to happen to me if someone finds out?* It wasn't until much later that I would find answers to any of these questions.

You may be wondering why the rapes abruptly came to an end. I have wondered the same question. I believed for years that she came to an epiphany that what she was doing was psychologically, physically, and morally damaging to someone she was supposed to love and protect, when the truth is much more logical and hurtful. I had become too old and was no longer useful. In two years, when this all began, I had gone from an eight-year-old child to a ten-year-old prepubescent boy with the possibility of getting my fifteen-year-old sister pregnant. Pregnancy meant being discovered, and this was something she could not allow to happen, so she told me it was wrong and brought it to an end, leaving me broken and confused with no understanding that incest had occurred, while allowing the thought that would mature into a belief that would eventually become a cold, hard fact: men can't be raped.[39]

---

39. Rogers, Jr., *Raped Black Male: A Memoir.*

PART THREE

THE ROAD OF TRIALS:
Grieving, anger, and understanding it was not your fault

In *Journey Into Mystery #83*, Doctor Donald Blake stumbles upon a wooden stick hidden in a cave in Norway. When struck by someone worthy, the stick transforms into the mythical hammer Mjolnir, and the stick's holder becomes Thor, the legendary god of thunder. In *Thor#159* "Who is the Real Don Blake," readers discover Donald Blake is worthy of possessing the power of Thor, because beneath the Donald Blake exterior is the god of thunder.

In the first few pages, Donald Blake appears distraught as he attempts to piece together the mystery of his existence and connection to the Norse god, Thor. On these first few pages Donald Blake lies awake in bed, thinking to himself, "My life as Thor began a few short years ago when I found the enchanted hammer! But Thor has lived for ages! So who was Thor before I found the mystic mallet? And who was Dr. Blake?"[40]

Thor's father Odin, who is the king of Asgard, reveals how Thor's headstrong and ignorant actions led him to create Donald Blake. The comic begins with the god of thunder violating a truce with the Storm Giants by venturing to the planet Niffleheim just for the sport of waging battle. After returning to Asgard, Thor starts a brawl with his fellow Asgardians, causing Odin to look unfavorably on his actions. He tells Thor, "Though thou art supreme in thy power, and thy pride, thou must know weakness, thou must feel pain!"[41] So, to teach Thor humility, Odin strips Thor of his powers and memories and sends the former god to Earth. When Thor lands, he is no longer a God. Instead, he is Donald Blake, a somewhat petite medical student in need of a cane due to a lame leg.

When Dr. Blake finally understands his connection to Thor, he slams his walking stick onto the floor and transforms into the superhero. With a smile and his magical mallet raised in the air, Thor says, "Though in spirit I am Donald Black, 'tis Thor that I have ever been! God of thunder now, and fore'er!"[42]

Thor's journey throughout *Thor* #159 depicts the Hero's Journey stage called **Road of Trials.** During the Road of Trials, the soon-to-be hero takes risks, makes mistakes, and gains experience. If this were a superhero movie, this stage would be a montage of the hero developing the perfect costume and learning to use their abilities in a humorous, but also dramatic, way that does not harm them or other innocent bystanders. While the Road of Trials is filled with mistakes, it is also where the hero gains wisdom. The Road of Trials is used to determine

---

40. Lee, Stan, and Kirby, *Thor* #159.

41. Lee, Stan, and Kirby,

42. Lee, Stan, and Kirby,

whether the subject is worthy of the transformation necessary to be called a hero. As a survivor, this does not mean determining whether or not you are worthy of healing, because you are. Instead, the Road of Trials means putting in the work to heal. This work takes the form of conscientiously recognizing and changing cognitive distortions, finding and maintaining a relationship with a therapist you trust, regularly meditating, and facing memories that may be difficult to confront, but are necessary to reconcile in order to heal.

Along the Road of Trials, the hero journeys into the **Abyss** where he experiences uncertainty, unease, and sadness. For Don Blake, this is when he struggles to understand and piece together the puzzle of his existence. While there are times of distress, there are also moments of **apotheosis** when the hero is filled with joy after accomplishing a difficult task. Survivors can experience this when they learn how to prevent themselves from dissociating or they piece together a memory that helps them to better understand the history of the abuse they suffered as a child. For Don Blake, apotheosis occurs when he realizes he and Thor are one and the same.

For a survivor, there is no short, humorous, five-minute montage from which the survivor understands the impact of their childhood trauma and is healed. Instead, the Road of Trials spans years of growth and patience as the survivor visits, explores, revisits, and evaluates the impact of their trauma on the past and present. Like a hero's road of trials, the survivor's is also filled with journeys into the abyss and moments of apotheosis.

Just as Don Blake questioned his connection to Thor, male survivors often question:

- whether or not their sexual abuse disqualifies them from

being a man.
- whether their sexual abuse determines their current sexual preferences.
- whether their sexual abuse means that they will one day become a perpetrator of childhood sexual abuse.

It's common for thoughts like these to circulate as male survivors attempt to remember their childhood trauma and understand the impact it has had on their current life. These worries can cause survivors to experience deep lulls of sadness and confusion. These periods are dark and seem to last an eternity as the puzzle pieces of the past slowly begin to fit together. When that happens, a survivor may experience brief moments of apotheosis. This part of the book explores the stage of the healing process when the survivor learns to grieve, feel, and express anger. It's also the stage when the survivor comes to understand that the childhood sexual abuse was not their fault.

CHAPTER NINE

Iron Man and Becoming the Villain

Tales of Suspense #39 reveals the birth of Tony Stark as Iron Man. In many ways, his origin story is like Jon Favreau's filmic depiction *Iron Man*. The only difference between the comic realm of Iron Man and the movie version is that the comic depicts the irrational, propagandized fear of Asian culture that was prevalent in 1950s and '60s America. While *Tales of Suspense* is set in the jungles of Vietnam, the movie depicts the villain in the caves of Afghanistan. Tony is there after being captured while selling weapons of war to the United States Army. In both the comic and movie versions, Tony has shrapnel from a bomb dangerously close to penetrating his heart. Both tellings have Tony Stark receiving medical help from an incarcerated ally. This ally is a genius, and when he dies, Tony vows to avenge his death. In both handlings, Tony builds an iron suit which he uses to escape, and then to fight crime as he strives to rid the world of evil.

For two decades, Tony Stark is successful as the comic book

hero Iron Man. He is an intelligent inventor who continuously improves the technology of Iron Man, defeats enemies, and brings together other heroes to reach their full potential in S.H.I.E.L.D. and the Avengers. However, in 1979, Tony faces a more deadly foe that threatens to destroy his success and that of Stark Enterprises: alcohol addiction. In *Iron Man #128* "Demon in a Bottle," Tony turns to alcohol to cope with the pressures of being Iron Man. He's accidentally killed a man; fired his trusted servant, Jarvis; and nearly lost control of Stark Enterprises.

Tony's addiction to alcohol can be used to help explain why survivors of childhood sexual abuse also frequently develop addictions, and his story offers some strategies for how to rise above the addiction.

Understanding Addiction and Self-Harm

Many survivors, at one point or another, turn to addiction and/or self-harm to cope with the effects of their sexual abuse. This happens because even if the survivor has made the decision to heal, the road of trials can be extremely challenging. Triggers cause memories to return and emotions to become overwhelming. When this occurs, survivors seek a means to numb their internal pain and to feel happier and more alive. Substances can seem like the answer. Unfortunately, addictions and self-harm affect the survivor's health and can cause death.

Addictions to drugs and/or alcohol are all too common among survivors. These addictions do not make you a bad person, but they can lead to habitual behaviors that are reminiscent of villains in comic books and victims in reality. These behaviors require the help and guidance of professionals in organizations such as Alcoholics Anonymous (AA), Al-Anon, Al-Ateen, therapy, and group counseling. This is not because individuals who have developed an addiction are not strong, but because getting help from those who have lived through similar trauma provides a new sense of support, and that's needed when the pain of the past becomes too overwhelming. It is a primary reason for the publication of this book: to provide male survivors with the strength to heal by letting them know they are not alone in their abuse.

To understand how addiction and self-harm can affect all types of individuals, whether they are rich, poor, or viewed by others or themselves as heroes or villains, we'll explore Tony Stark's addiction. Even heroes can sometimes stray.

Tony Stark and Alcohol Addiction

Iron Man #128 "Demon in a Bottle" begins by exploring the limits of heroes and men when it states:

> By definition, a hero is a man who battles against overwhelming odds for a cause, an ideal, or for the lives of innocents. The cause and ideal may vary with the moving headlines, while the innocents, in today's world of muddy morality, may ultimately prove to be the guilty. Which leaves but one constant in the definition: that a hero is, above all, a man...a man subject to pressures and responsibility far beyond those of his peers. Such a burden must take its toll, eventually, from even the most valiant warrior. And it is then that the test of a true hero

begins.[43]

While there are some problems with this excerpt, there is some truth to it as well. No matter who the hero may be, there is no way he can cope with the pressures of life and trauma alone. If an individual believes they can do it all alone, life becomes too overwhelming, and with enough pressure, the stresses of life have the possibility of leading to addiction. This is the lesson Tony must learn as he stares at the headline of a newspaper labeling Iron Man a murderer, and takes stock of the assets and friends he has lost on his journey to becoming a superhero. Tony sits at his desk in a high-rise, overlooking the city. He's wearing his Iron Man suit. Beside him sits a mostly empty bottle of alcohol, a completely empty bottle of alcohol, and his Iron Man helmet. Before declaring he will no longer be Tony Stark but instead will be Iron Man on a full-time basis, he takes a shot of whiskey to finish the bottle. While drunk, Tony fastens the Iron Man helmet on his head and flies into the sky, crashing through the window of his high-rise office.

He doesn't realize he forgot to open the window until he's shattered the glass. Inebriated and zigzagging across the sky, Iron Man discovers a derailed train car filled with chlorine gas. No one has died, and the authorities have the situation under control, but because his judgment is impaired, Iron Man decides to take matters into his own hands. Cocky, drunk, and in corny superhero fashion, he asks a police officer, "Mind if I save the day?"[44] and proceeds to lift the derailed train cars into the air. Unfortunately, the hero's irrational actions lead to him bending and breaking the connecting bars of the train.

---

43. Layton, Michelinie, Romita Sr., *Iron Man #128*.

44. Layton, Michelinie, Romita Sr.,

This sends the train tumbling to the ground. On impact, the deadly chlorine gas fills the air, causing an emergency evacuation of a five-mile radius. With angry fists and damning fingers pointed toward the sky, Stark realizes his mistake and flies away.

The hero lands on the roof of his building, enters his home, and throws his helmet across the room frustrated with the thought that he cannot do anything right. He's been unable to design and create anything new, and full of frustration and self-pity, he pours himself a drink. However, before he can put the alcohol to his lips, a woman takes his glass and pushes the drink away. Her name is Bethany Cabe. She's Stark's current girlfriend, and she tells Tony she is there to help as a friend. Tony tells her, "I can handle things myself,"[45] as he snatches his hand away and finishes preparing his drink. Before Tony has the opportunity to drink the alcohol, Beth proceeds to tell Tony about her previous life and her late husband, Alexander van Tilberg, a West German Junior Ambassador to the U.S. She explains how Alex loved his job, but became addicted to pills...to sleep, to stay awake, and to escape its pressures. When Beth tried to talk to him about it, he became angry and said he could handle it on his own, so she left. Alex died a month later when his car ran off the road after a heart attack. Beth tells Tony she believes that if she had stayed, maybe Alex would be alive. She tells Tony to not feel sorry for her or himself. She says:

> "Can't you see? You're becoming your own worst enemy! And you're trying to kill that enemy with a bottle as surely as Alex did with pills and a car! Only I'm not

45. Layton, Michelinie, Romita Sr.,

turning away this time. I know you've got pressures you can't tell to anyone, but for God's sake let go of the troubles you can talk about! You've got friends—Me, Rhody, Scott—friends who care about you. So stop playing the self-sacrificing lover and share your life! Let us help you! Blast it, Tony, open up and get some of that weight off your shoulders before it breaks you!"[46]

Tony listens to all this while staring out the window, sweating, with tears running down his face. Beth believes her story has fallen on deaf ears, and just before walking away, Tony asks for help.

What is most impressive about Beth's monologue to Tony is that every word is true for survivors, and many males in general. As discussed previously, because of toxic masculinity, many men believe they must carry the weight of the world on their shoulders. They believe they are not allowed to share their emotions, which, unfortunately, means they feel as though they cannot share their life. They feel alone, and the only way to manage these feelings of loneliness, isolation, depression, and anxiety is through drugs and alcohol, rather than by leaning on friends, family, and professionals who can give them the help they need. This is the problem with deciding to manage everything alone: it leaves the person incapable of asking for help because that person starts to view help as a sign of weakness. As a male survivor, it is important to remember that you do not want to be a hero. You want to be better than a hero. Recover, heal, and become the complete person you were meant to be. Become a survivor.

In the '70s, as with the opioid epidemic now, addiction

46. Layton, Michelinie, Romita Sr.,

was everywhere, and drugs were a major topic of discussion. Artists and writers used the medium of comic books to reach young people before they became addicted. Unfortunately, many comics glossed over the rocky road to recovery, centering their attention on only the effects of the addiction. However, *Iron Man #128* is different. Where most comics would come to an end, "Demon in a Bottle" expands and discusses how Tony's addiction does not vanish overnight. In fact, they explain how battling the addiction is a constant struggle for Tony. After Tony asks Beth for help, there are images of Tony getting angry at Beth and begging for a single drink. These are beside other images of him struggling to create new inventions and crying his heart out while kneeling at Beth's feet. Later, David Micheline and Bob Layton write:

> In modern times, addiction withdrawal has come to be thought of in animal terms: "Monkey on my back," "Cold turkey," etc. And Bethany Cabe soon learns why as she listens to a mature, sophisticated playboy's dog-like whimpers, his pleas for, "Just one drink"—and then suffers his feral anger and abuse when she refuses. For days the stalemate rages—until at long last, emotional blocks begin to crack, then crumble, and Tony Stark spills his pent-up pain like milk from a split pail. He sighs, he shudders...and he shares. The purging helps with encouragement, he returns to his life's work. And though the lines occasionally squirm and curve even when etched carefully with a T-Square—it is in the end, a beginning.[47]

---

47. Layton, Michelinie, Romita Sr.,

Even by today's standards, this is where most readers would expect the comic to end. But the comic continues to defy expectations. It continues for eight additional pages. Here, readers realize that Tony's addiction will be part of his story for the remainder of his life. It does not end. As with all addictions, it lingers and strikes when at his lowest.

The story continues with Tony apologizing to Jarvis, his butler, and learning that Jarvis sold his two shares of Stark International because he needed the money to pay for his mother's medical bills. Selling those two shares gives S.H.I.E.L.D. controlling interest of the company. Jarvis tries to retrieve the shares but is unsuccessful. Tony even becomes Iron Man and smashes the office of the businessman, but it is too late. The shares were sold. Dejected, hopeless, and feeling as though he has no other options, Tony returns home and begins to prepare himself a drink. Bethany and Jarvis watch in horror, pleading for him to put the bottle down. Tony's reply to his friends is simply, "What else matters?"[48] He believes he has lost it all and the only option remaining lies at the bottom of a whiskey bottle. Bethany asks Tony to consider his employees, friends, her, and his dreams. She pleads but leaves Tony to make the decision. Bethany and Jarvis begin to leave as Tony sweats bullets and decides between the dream or the drink. Shaking, he puts the top on the bottle and makes the decision to remain sober.

While not perfect, the story does an excellent job of explaining how addiction impacts a person's life, no matter who they are, or how strong they believe themselves to be. Tony's addiction to alcohol is another example of how heroes some-

---

48. Layton, Michelinie, Romita Sr.,

times fall and how the expectations and stereotypes we have about addiction can negatively impact those closest to us. Comics that address societal issues are not perfect, but they let individuals who are addicted to drugs or alcohol know that addiction can happen to even the best people, with the best of intentions, and that it can transform heroes into villains. For surviors, becoming addicted to drugs and alcohol are temporary fixes to numb the pain, but they have the potential to cause premature death.

Any addiction, trauma, or abuse cannot be conquered alone. Find support and lean on those closest to you until you can stand on your own and be the support needed for someone else. If you attempt to conquer your addiction alone, you will fail, and the cycle will continue. If you don't seek help for the trauma, you run the risk of succumbing to addiction. And if you have not become addicted to drugs or alcohol following a traumatic event, consider yourself blessed. Don't judge others and their ability or inability to cope. These thoughts can cause you to become the villain in another person's story. Instead, attempt to be the change you wish to see in the world. It's only then we will all find the strength needed to heal.

CHAPTER TEN

The Hulk, Learning to Grieve, and Accepting All Emotions

In *The Incredible Hulk #1* readers are introduced to Dr. Bruce Banner and the brutish Hulk that lies waiting just beneath his surface. In this comic, Dr. Banner is working in a military compound in the desert to develop a gamma-radiation bomb for the United States Army. Moments before testing the device, a teenage boy named Rick Jones rolls onto the site in a red hot rod. Afraid for the boy's life, Bruce takes a jeep and races into the desert to save the teenager's life. With only moments to spare, Banner manages to pull the boy from his car and fling him into a nearby ditch. Unfortunately, Banner cannot follow the boy to the ditch in time, and when the bomb explodes, Bruce Banner is bombarded with gamma radiation. When Bruce awakes hours later, he and the teenage boy are safe in a secure bunker far from the detonation site.

At first, all seems well. Neither Bruce nor the teenager seem to be harmed in any way. However, as the sun sets and the moon begins to rise, Bruce transforms. Soon, in place of a brilliant scientist, there stands a gray-skinned Goliath (the original Hulk was gray, not green) who reacts on instinct rather than logic. With superhuman strength, the monster becomes filled with rage, breaks down the wall of the bunker, and demolishes a military jeep before walking off into the desert. This is the moment the incredible Hulk is born.

On the surface, it may seem as though Stan Lee and Jack Kirby merely developed a modern retelling of Robert Louis Stevenson's Dr. Jekyll and Mr. Hyde, but the Hulk's origin tale is more than a monster story. It is a story of childhood trauma and the suppression of emotions to feel safe and in control. The Hulk's origins—his tragic childhood and abusive father—can help you understand the anger and grief you experience as a survivor of childhood sexual abuse. However, we must first explore why survivors may fear their emotions and attempt to suppress them.

Why Survivors Fear Grieving and Anger

As a male survivor, you may have come to fear your emotions. This may be because emotions were a source of pain in an already traumatic world. Or it may be that following your trauma, you had limited access to any and all of your emotions. While avoiding emotions may have allowed you to survive the trauma of your sexual abuse as a child, as an adult this same behavior limits your interactions and the strength of your relationships with people you love.

One emotion you may be afraid to express is anger, as you may live in fear of what anger could make you do. Pushing this emotion away is the same behavior a superhero shows when they put the needs and wants of others before themselves.

However, anger, along with all your other emotions, is beneficial and crucial to healing. While you may fear expressing your anger, anger is healthy. In fact, it's critical that you can have anger toward your abuser and those who did not protect you as a child when you were their responsibility. Without admitting this anger, you will never be able to reach a resolution and move on.

While anger is an important emotion to express, to move forward through the healing process, it is also vital to grieve and mourn the things that were lost or taken away when the sexual abuse occurred. This means feeling more than sadness over this horrific event; you can feel sorrowful for the lasting effects the sexual abuse had on your life.

As a survivor, there are likely experiences you never got to have. You may not have been able to give your virginity willingly and to someone you care for. You may not have known what it means to grow up in a stable home. Questions concerning the direction of your life and the people you loved will arise as you move throughout your journey of healing, causing you to mourn the life and happiness you could have had.

Unfortunately, these parts of your life cannot be reclaimed, and the questions about what could have been cannot be answered. This is a fact that cannot be altered, and the pain of that truth is tangible, real, and deserving to be acknowledged. Grief over these things can occur numerous times throughout your journey as more memories surface and the truth of your sexual abuse becomes revealed. Do not rush the grieving process. Let it walk in tandem with the anger you have. Allow your grieving process the time it needs to become fully understood and mended.

The connection between grief, anger, and suppression of emotions can be understood by analyzing Banner and Hulk, and the defense mechanisms this character is using to feel safe and protected in an unsafe environment.

The Incredible Hulk and Understanding Internal Family Systems (IFS)

In *The Incredible Hulk #308* "And Here There Be Demons," three beings materialize, seemingly from thin air, to wake the Hulk and protect him from being ambushed. These beings appear only to be able to be seen and heard by the brutish Mean Green Machine. The first character's name is Guardian. In appearance, Guardian resembles an elf or sprite and carries a bow with a quiver of arrows. The other character is known as Goblin and resembles a blue demon with red eyes, long claws, and a whip-like tail. The final character's name is Glow and appears to be a sentient purple star. When the Hulk wakes, the creatures disappear.

At the end of the comic, the characters reappear and help the Hulk escape a horde of purple demons and a former friend who's become an enemy. When the Hulk is safe but sad that he is alone in a strange crossroads dimension without a way to get home, the creatures collectively tell the Hulk, "You ain't alone Greenface. Cheer up! You'll never be alone again, Hulk. Not as long as you have us! And I daresay that you shall always have us."[49]

Throughout the next two issues of *The Incredible Hulk,* Guardian, Goblin, and Glow exist within the Hulk and Bruce Banner's consciousness, and each is responsible for keeping the Hulk and Banner safe from harm. The Guardian protects

_____

49. Mantlo, Buscema, *The Incredible Hulk # 308.*

by providing rational thought designed to ensure the Hulk and Banner's safety, well-being, and self-preservation. Guardian accomplishes this task by shooting an arrow charged with energy from Glow. Glow has the ability to make Hulk and Banner feel safe and capable so that they can think rationally. Goblin, on the other hand, pushes the Hulk and Banner to feel anger and fear so that they'll fight for survival rather than remain passive. During different moments of conflict, either Guardian, Goblin, or Glow take control to provide the Hulk and Banner with the tools they need for survival.

Although Guardian, Goblin, and Glow are fictional characters, they can help illuminate a survivor's need to either *fight*, *flight*, or *freeze* to survive dangerous situations. Bessel van Der Kolk, M.D. explains in *The Body Keeps the Score* that when faced with danger, an individual has three primary options. The first is to either fight off the threat (fight) or run for safety (flight). The other option is for the individual to preserve themselves "by shutting down and expending as little energy as possible." This is known as freezing or collapsing. Guardian, Goblin, and Glow represent an individual's ability to fight, flight, or freeze. In the same way the Hulk and Banner have Guardian, Goblin, and Glow to help them navigate dangerous situations, survivors have the ability to either fight for their escape, possess the rational capacity to run away, or know the only way to survive is by remaining still and allowing the threat to pass. The survivor's actions or inactions help to ensure their survival in the same way Guardian, Goblin, and Glow ensure the survival of the Hulk and Banner.

These three characters also exemplify **internal family system therapy (IFS),** a form of therapy that may help you, as a survivor, understand and heal from your childhood trauma. IFS was developed by Dr. Richard Schwartz in the

1980s. Arielle Schwartz, PhD, explains in *The Complex PTSD Workbook* that individuals have different parts of themselves that hold different emotions. As a survivor, these different parts help to keep you, the Self, safe. Some of these parts are viewed as acceptable (**Managers** and **Firefighters**) while others are viewed negatively (**Exiles**). Schwartz states how "the goal of IFS therapy is to develop your relationship to the Self," which Dr. Schwartz describes as the core of who you are. "When you are living from this center, you have the capacity to be calm, confident, and compassionate."[50]

When analyzing the Hulk's consciousness from the lens of IFS, Glow, Guardian, and Goblin represent the Manager, Firefighter, and Exile of a survivor's personality. Glow embodies the Manager because Glow provides the Hulk and Banner with the capacity to feel safe and think rationally. Guardian embodies the Firefighter of a survivor's personality because Guardian suppresses the irrational actions of the Goblin in the same way Firefighters suppress the escape of Exiles. Finally, Goblin embodies the Exile of a survivor's personality because Goblin reacts on instinct. He unleashes emotions you are attempting to suppress, such as anger and fear, in the same way that Exiles unleash emotions and memories that a survivor has tried to lock away.

Alone, neither Glow, Guardian, nor Goblin can protect the Hulk and Banner from harm, just as Managers, Firefighters, and Exiles are not adequate alone. However, together they protect the survivor and allow him the safety of experiencing and feeling all his emotions. *The Incredible Hulk #312* "Monster" offers insight into how this is possible.

---

50. Schwartz PhD, *The Complex PTSD Workbook*.

"Monster" explains how Bruce Banner's father, Brian Banner, was an abusive, narcissistic, alcoholic who believed his son was a monster, and murdered his wife, Rebecca Banner, when Bruce was a boy. Throughout Bruce's childhood, Brian Banner treated him as nothing more than a burden who had prevented him from having a happy marriage with his wife. Rather than allow Rebecca Banner the opportunity to raise and love her son, he forced Bruce to be raised by Nurse Meachum, an abusive, neglectful live-in nanny. Throughout the comic, the characters who threaten Bruce and cause him to feel fear and anger (Brian Banner, Nurse Meachum, and General Ross) transform into the red-eyed, blue-skinned demon, Goblin, who later becomes part of Bruce's subconscious.

The only person who showed Bruce any love as a child was his mother. She provided her son with the future protectors of his subconscious, Guardian and Glow. As a baby, she gave Bruce a stuffed doll that resembled an elf which he named Guardian because it provided him with protection when she was gone. Above his crib (the one place he felt safe from Nurse Meachum) and on the Christmas tree, was Glow, shining down, providing Bruce with feelings of safety and comfort. Glow also appears beside the image of his future wife, Betty Ross, allowing him to feel love and affection for her.

Prior to the explosion of the gamma radiation bomb that unleashed the Hulk from Bruce Banner, Guardian, Goblin, and Glow each acted separately to protect Bruce. As the Hulk, these creatures took form in his subconscious to provide protection in the same way they provided protection for Bruce as a child. However, it is not until the end of the comic when Guardian, Goblin, and Glow come together that the Hulk is able to calm himself, transform back into Bruce Banner, and begin to grieve the life he was never able to live due to his traumatic childhood. Prior to uniting into one beam of light to calm the Hulk, each contributes to the conversation when they say,

> "Hurt so often as a child, Bruce Banner learned to live inside himself, never to let us—his reason, his rage, and his desire for survival—out! Perhaps he might have, given time. Given help. But then the gamma bomb took the man molded from a twisted child and transformed him into the very monster his father had always predicted he'd become…The truth may not make him happy, but at least he is short o' dyin! An' that means he's ready t' come out from hidin inside the Hulk an' reclaim his life again!"[51]

Like Bruce Banner facing the reality of his childhood trauma, you must face and accept that your childhood may not have been pleasant either. Accepting this truth may be painful, but you do not have to hide behind your inner Hulk. You can and should feel all your emotions. Allowing yourself to remember and heal from the past will allow you to become your best self and become truly intimate with those you care for without fear of hurting them with your rage.

"Monster" showcases anger as a normal emotion that cannot be suppressed forever and cannot be perpetually used as a source of motivation. Eventually, memories of the past must be allowed to return, fear must be confronted, rage must be accepted, and grieving must take place. It is the only way true healing can occur. Just as Guardian, Goblin, and Glow come together to calm the Hulk, your Man-

---

51. Mantlo, Mignola, *The Incredible Hulk #312*.

ager, Firefighter, and Exile must learn to accept one another to continue your progression along the survivor's journey of healing. With help, you can become more than a raging Hulk. You can become a survivor and an overcomer.

Subjective Units of Distress Scales and Safety

For the majority of Bruce Banner's life, he has lived in a constant state of fear, fear of his father when he was a boy, and fear of his emotions after the explosion of the gamma radiation bomb. Living in a constant state of fear can also be said for many male survivors of childhood sexual abuse. While Bruce Banner is afraid of becoming an unstoppable brute capable of hurting those he cares for, male survivors are afraid for different reasons.

Many male survivors find it difficult to trust others out of fear of being hurt in the same manner they were hurt by their abuser. Male survivors do not trust their thoughts due to the shame perpetuated by society that because they are boys and men they cannot be sexually abused, assaulted, or raped. Their mistrust is compounded by their belief that they were betrayed by their body when they reacted to physical stimuli, which may have resulted in an erection or ejaculation.

A male survivor lives in a constant state of fear in and around his body, much like how Bruce Banner lives after his exposure to gamma radiation. To establish a sense of safety, some male survivors develop a Bruce-Banner façade where they attempt to numb themselves to emotions in the hope that they do not lose control of their emotions and become the villain they believe themselves to be. Remember, that belief comes from the shame associated with being a male survivor. Unfortunately, when the façade is broken and their bottled emotions are released, their expressions of anger, fear, and anxiety cause them to believe they are the villain they feared themselves to be. The only way to conquer the need to live behind this façade is to learn to identify and feel a full range of emotions. One tool to help accomplish this task is the use of the **subjective units of distress (SUD) scale**. Developed by Dr. Larry Smyth, the scale has eleven points and is a simple way to communicate your level of distress, safety, and anxiety to yourself or when speaking with a therapist, counselor, or psychiatrist.

Although fundamentally the same, there are two different ways in which the SUD scale can be interpreted. The first SUD scale progresses from 0-10, increasing from feelings of calm and relaxation on the first half of the scale to overwhelming emotions of fear, anxiety, and anger on the latter half of the scale. With this SUD scale, the goal is to remain on the first half of the scale since this is where you feel calm and in control.

The SUD scale was later modified for survivors of complex PTSD to lead from feelings of numbness when at a ranking of *zero* to *four*, or extreme rage when at a ranking of *six* to *ten*, to a safe regulation of emotions when at a ranking of *five*. With this second SUD scale, the goal is not to achieve a feeling of numbness with a ranking of zero or a cascade of paralyzing emotions ranging from rage to distress and shame with a ranking of ten. Instead, the goal is to feel emotions, but be able to manage and express them in a healthy manner with a ranking of four, five, or six.

Reaching either a ranking of 1-4 on the first SUD scale or 4-6 on the second SUD scale takes time, practice, and work. The goal is to recognize and feel emotions, rather than to keep them suppressed so that when you experience feelings, they do not control your actions.

Below are two different SUD scales to help you better understand and navigate the emotions you may feel as you progress along your survivor's journey of healing. To help you better understand and enjoy the scales, each level of the SUD scale is explained through the lens of Bruce Banner and the Hulk, their capacity to feel their emotions, and the impact those emotions have on the characters' actions. Use these scales with your therapist, counselor, or psychiatrist to reach a place where emotions feel safe.

BANNER/HULK SUDS SCALE #1	
Numeric Rating	Description
Zero	You feel like Bruce Banner when he's alone in his lab prior to being exposed to the gamma-radiation bomb. You are at peace. You feel completely relaxed, almost as if you are in a deep, dreamless sleep. You have no distress, anxiety, or discomfort at all.
One	You feel like Bruce Banner when he's alone with his wife, Betty Ross, prior to being exposed to the gamma-radiation bomb. You feel at ease. Able to be yourself. You are awake, but not hypervigilant. Your mind wanders and drifts, similarly to how you feel just prior to falling asleep.
Two	You feel like Bruce Banner when he's alone in his apartment after a long day of work, prior to being exposed to the gamma-radiation bomb. You feel fulfilled, relaxed, and comfortable. You know you are in a safe place physically, mentally, and emotionally. You may feel this way when you are at home watching television, reading a comic, or relaxing on a calm afternoon.

Three	You feel like Bruce Banner at work, but not when he's under a strict deadline. This is still prior to his exposure to the gamma-radiation bomb. You feel like yourself, but you also feel you have to keep a façade so you don't become too frustrated or lose your temper. You feel some anxiety. It's nothing too severe, but it's also not pleasant.
Four	You feel like Bruce Banner while he's working under a strict deadline and dealing with the temper of General Ross. This is still prior to his exposure to the gamma-radiation bomb. General Ross's yelling makes it difficult for you to focus and control your rage. You are uncomfortable, anxious, and angry, but the emotions are manageable.
Five	You feel like Bruce Banner after being exposed to the gamma-radiation bomb. The Hulk has not emerged to assume control, but you feel his rage and anger growing just beneath the surface. With enough focus, the brute can be contained and your feelings can be managed without losing control. At any moment, though, the scales could tip in either direction.
Six	You feel like Bruce Banner as he is beginning to transform into the Hulk. You know the feelings of anger, anxiety, fear, and frustration can no longer be contained. Similar to Bruce, you have unpleasant feelings of worry and apprehension as your ability to think rationally fades. But for the time being, you are capable of not reacting purely on instinct.
Seven	You feel like the Hulk when he is alone and not under the immediate threat of attack. You feel anger, frustration, and fear, but you are unable to identify why. The rationality of Bruce exists in the background of your thoughts, so you're capable of controlling some actions, but the Hulk leads.
Eight	You feel like the Hulk when he has assumed full control of Bruce Banner's mind and body. The rationality of Bruce is a distant echo. Thinking and problem solving are extremely difficult. Your bodily distress is substantial. You feel uncontrollable emotions, and they make your ability to complete everyday functions difficult.

Nine	You feel like the Hulk when in the middle of battle. The high levels of extreme distress make it nearly impossible for you to think clearly. Like the Hulk, you are reacting on instinct and attempting to fight or flee a dangerous situation.
Ten	You feel like the Hulk when Bruce Banner has been completely separated from the brute and exists as a completely different person. When this occurs, there is no rationality to your thoughts. Friends and foes are one and the same. The feelings of anxiety, fear, and rage are beyond comprehension. Like the Hulk, you are blind to rational thought. There is only the desire for safety, control, and dominance.

BANNER/HULK SUDS SCALE #2	
Numeric Rating	**Description**
0-2	When experiencing a 0-2 on the SUD scale, your ability to feel and express emotion has been drained over time due to the duration of your abuse. The prolonged physical and psychological pain of being sexually abused makes you feel as though your emotions are dead. This fear of feeling any emotion is like Bruce Banner when he's already been exposed to the gamma-radiation bomb, and tries to numb himself to feelings so that he does not unleash Hulk. The impact of your childhood trauma and the bombardment of overwhelming experiences causes you to dissociate from feeling any emotion, including pain.

| 3 | When experiencing a three on the SUD scale, you ignore your feelings for the benefit of others, or mirror the emotions of others to please those around you. You either do not know how to have feelings of your own, or you believe accommodating the needs and wants of others is the only way to feel safe. You may better understand this level of the SUDS scale if it is viewed through the lens of Bruce Banner as a boy. While living in the same house as his father and Nurse Meachum, he had no ability to fight or flight to safety. So, Bruce had to either freeze or fawn. This meant he could remain still and hidden until the danger passed, or he could attempt to please his abuser to limit the abuse he was forced to endure. Although this ability may have ensured your survival in the same way it kept Bruce safe from harm, these loose boundaries as an adult can cause you to ignore your own feelings and to put the needs and wants of others before your own. While this may eliminate feelings of shame associated with your childhood trauma, it can lead to burnout. |
| 4-6 | When experiencing a 4-6 on the SUD scale, you have learned to maintain a balance between feeling and controlling your emotions rather than allowing them to control you. While four and six are good scores on the SUDS scale, and demonstrate your ability to feel and simultaneously remain in control of your emotions, the optimal score is five. Experiencing emotions while at a five is similar to Hulk and Bruce Banner each having a hand on the steering wheel and sharing control. When this occurs, both Bruce and the Hulk can feel their emotions and think rationally so they do not shut down or lose control. In this stage, you feel safe, strong, capable, and no longer afraid of hurting those you care for when attending to your needs and emotions. Achieving a five on the SUD scale means feeling a range of emotions while having the ability to not let them overwhelm you. It means feeling human and having the ability to manage your emotions. You are not impenetrable to emotion the way Hulk is impenetrable to bullets and bombs. |

7	Experiencing a seven on the SUD scale means that instead of attempting to please and attend to the needs of others, you're becoming hedonistic. This means you are primarily concerned with only your own emotions and have little-to-no regard for the feelings of others. This is akin to the Hulk experiencing tunnel vision and being concerned only with his desire to feel happy, safe, or less frightened. Just as a baby lacks the empathy necessary to worry about the welfare of others, the Hulk and you at 7 on the SUD scale care only for your own needs.
8-10	Experiencing an 8-10 on the SUD scale is when emotions overwhelm to the point of explosive anger, crippling anxiety, shame, and/or guilt. Here, emotions have become out of control in the same way the Hulk becomes out of control when severed completely from Bruce Banner. Rather than possessing any form of rational thought, you react on instinct. Your emotions are in control of you rather than the opposite.

It is important to know that although anger is normal and healthy, there are still healthy and unhealthy ways of expressing anger. Use this guide to help understand how to express and relieve anger constructively:

- Do not hurt yourself or anyone else
- Do not destroy property unless it is owned by you and designated to be able to be destroyed
- Do not imagine hurting yourself
- You can scream
- You can punch a pillow or punching bag
- You can write a letter and burn it
- You can run
- You can do other exercises

It is important to understand that there is no such thing as a negative emotion. All emotions are healthy if expressed in a healthy manner. The key is knowing how to control them rather than allowing them to control you. Learning how to accomplish this does not happen overnight. It takes time, patience, and work to develop the confidence necessary to fail, learn, and try again. Growth is the goal, not perfection.

CHAPTER ELEVEN

Understanding It Wasn't Your Fault

This stage in the healing process may be the longest and most difficult for any survivor of sexual abuse, but it can be especially hard for male survivors. One primary reason is that many people of all genders are convinced males cannot be sexually assaulted or raped. Depending on the nature of the sexual abuse, some male survivors think, "If I did not want to have sex, then why did I have an erection?" or "why did some parts of the sexual abuse feel good?"

No matter the sexual abuse, there is no way to control the body's reaction to certain stimulations. If you were placed in a sexually abusive situation, you do not carry the blame, regardless of your bodily responses; being placed in that situation makes you the victim. You can come to understand this through **cognitive behavior therapy (CBT)**. CBT is a form of therapy that recognizes the connection between an individual's thoughts, behaviors, and the way in which they feel. CBT works to help individuals who suffer from problems such as depression or addiction to free their thoughts of **cognitive distortions**. In effect, you are changing your behaviors by altering your automatic thoughts, and this also helps you change the way you feel. The cognitive distortions that will be explored in this chapter are:

- **All-or-Nothing Thinking**
- **Should/Shouldn't Have Statements**
- **Jumping to Conclusions**
  - **Mind Reading**
  - **Fortune Telling**
- **Personalization/Blame**

This chapter explores these cognitive distortions and their impact on you believing that the childhood sexual abuse was your fault. Jeph Loeb and Tim Sale's color comics, *Daredevil: Yellow; Captain America: White; Hulk: Gray;* and *Spider-Man: Blue* will be used throughout this chapter to analyze, understand, and apply these cognitive distortions.

Jeph Loeb and Tim Sale are very much the modern version of Stan Lee and Jack Kirby in that one name is often accompanied by the other. Loeb's artistry and Sale's narratives combine to tell stories in unparalleled ways. While the two creators are best known for the graphic novel *Batman: The Long Halloween,* their color comics utilize similarly unique graphics and simplistic storytelling to deliver their one-of-a-kind style. Each version of Loeb and Sale's color comics retells the origin of the heroes Daredevil, Captain America, the Hulk, and Spider-Man, but from the lens of the hero looking back with a sense of regret for their inability to save the person they either loved or cared for.

Daredevil: Yellow and Mind Reading

When Daredevil first appeared in 1964 in *Daredevil #1*, the hero's costume was not the crimson red color it is today. Instead, it was primarily yellow with a black vest, red gloves, and red boots. This is not because artist Bill Everett was confused about what color to make Daredevil, but because the hero's alter ego Matt Murdock created the costume from his murdered father's heavy-weight boxing shorts and robe. His father had been killed for not throwing a fight. *Daredevil: Yellow* explores Matt Murdock's journey to becoming Daredevil through a series of letters he writes to the deceased love of his life, Karen Page.

In this graphic novel, Matt is looking back at the beginning of his journey, trying to forgive himself for being unable to save Karen's life. Through his letters, he is also trying to remember the events that transformed him into the hero and man he became.

Although letter writing is an excellent way to progress along the healing process, Matt's words are laced with cognitive distortions. These prevent him from truly forgiving himself and appreciating that Karen's death was not his fault. Examining Matt's cognitive distortions can help you understand and change your negative automatic thoughts. This will help you switch your cognitively distorted thoughts into beneficial true statements.

The cognitive distortion exhibited most by Matt is **mind reading**. Mind reading is when a survivor attempts to predict the actions of others to feel more in control of his own life. When mind reading, survivors often assume others view them negatively, even if there's no definitive evidence for those thoughts. Daredevil has the super ability to sense things others are incapable of comprehending in the same way survivors who mindread believe they know what others are thinking.

Matt Murdock was blinded as a child, and the accident heightened his other senses. For example, Daredevil's hearing is so precise that he can hear when a villain's heart skips a beat moments before they pull the trigger of a gun. This superpower provides him time to avoid the bullet. He can smell an individual's cologne, perfume, or sweat, to know the person's location in a pitch-black room. Furthermore, the way sound reverberates off objects creates a form of echolocation that allows Daredevil to move through dark spaces with ease. All these abilities paint a picture of the world that is detailed beyond description.

As a survivor, your childhood abuse may have similarly turned your senses to eleven. Rather than detecting when someone's heart skips a beat, you may have the ability to detect when someone is upset, frustrated, or angry. Judith Herman explains this in her book *Trauma and Recovery* when she states, "To the chronically traumatized person, any action has potentially dire consequences. There is no room for mistakes."[52] Bessel van der Kolk provides further explanation when he states in *The Body Keeps the Score*, "for abused children, the whole world is filled with triggers. As long as they can imagine only disastrous outcomes to relatively benign situations, any image on a screen or on a billboard might be perceived as a harbinger of catastrophe."[53] Mind reading allows survivors to anticipate the thoughts, needs, and actions of those around them. Survivors then attempt to become what is wanted of them, rather than listening to what they themselves

---

52. Herman, *Trauma and Recovery*.
53. Kolk, van der., *The Body Keeps the Score*.

want.

As a child, mind reading may have been used to help predict when future abuses would take place. However, as an
adult who is now safe and beginning the process of healing,
mind reading can become a hindrance. It can impede your
ability to no longer feel ashamed or at fault for the sexual
abuse. Matt Murdock demonstrates how this perceived super
ability of mind reading can have a negative effect when his
overreliance on these abilities makes him forget he is human
and therefore capable of making mistakes. He takes for grant-
ed that he is incapable of fully knowing an individual's mind
without explicitly communicating with them. This is seen in
the second issue of *Daredevil: Yellow* when Matt narrates,
"My dad had won his tenth consecutive fight—ever since he
signed with a new manager named 'Sweeney.' Sweeny had a
nickname, too. 'The Fixer.' A fight manager named 'The Fixer'
and my dad, over-the-hill when he was forty, kept winning. I
can't imagine which one of us was more blind."[54] Here, although Matt has super abilities, we're told he's still a human
capable of making mistakes.

Mind reading prevents individuals from having tough conversations and expressing true intimacy because the person
doing the mind reading believes he knows implicitly what the
other person wants. This behavior is a reaction to fear. It's
born of the fear of what an abuser would do if the survivor
decided to take care of his own needs rather than remain hy-
per-focused on their abuser's.

Matt expresses the same sentiment in *Daredevil: Yellow* #4
when he states, "I was so blind, Karen. I could sense things no

---

54. Loeb, Sale, *Daredevil: Yellow.*

other person could, but on this one subject I was in the dark." [55]
Here, in this scene, Matt knows he has heightened senses, but
he is ignorant of the love his friend and law partner Foggy feels
for Karen Page. Mind reading as an adult can create blind
spots in your ability to read and communicate with individuals
you feel comfortable and safe around. It causes you to inadver-
tently ignore their needs, which, in turn, pushes them away.

To prevent yourself from mind reading, you must learn
skills to properly communicate, understand, and navigate your
own emotions while accepting that your needs are just as important as everyone else's.

Captain America: White and Should/Shouldn't Have Statements

Captain America is known as the First Avenger. After defeating
the villain, Red Skull, during World War II, Captain America's
plane crashed into the icy Atlantic Ocean and he was frozen
alive. Decades later, when Captain America's body was found
fully preserved and he was revived, he joined Iron Man, Thor,
and the Hulk to continue to protect America and its interests.
However, *Captain America: White* is less about Steve Rogers'
ascension to become Captain America, and more about how a
teenager and orphan named James Buchanan Barnes became
Captain America's sidekick, Bucky.

The series begins with Steve Rogers waking up in the future
and realizing not only that World War II is over but that everyone he has known and loved is dead. This includes his sidekick
Bucky. Steve Rogers does not write apologetic letters to Bucky

---

55. Loeb, Sale,

the way Daredevil does to Karen. Instead, Steve Rogers speaks to the memory of Bucky as if he is praying for forgiveness. Steve is filled with remorse and regret for Bucky's death, and his words are laced with cognitive distortions like Daredevil's when he's remembering Karen. *Captain America: White* primarily displays the cognitive distortion of **should/shouldn't have statements**.

When making should or shouldn't have statements, the survivor criticizes themselves and their actions by using "should," "ought to," "must," and "have to" statements. This distortion places unwarranted stress on the survivor about what they *must have* or *shouldn't have* done. It allows the survivor to abuse themselves verbally and no longer view themselves as human as they say things to themselves they would never say to their worst enemy. This reaffirms a survivor's feelings of worthlessness and reiterates their false belief that the abuse was their fault. Should/shouldn't have statements strip survivors of their sense of safety, making them feel weak. Captain America displays this cognitive distortion when he wakes up in the future and thinks back to his time in World War II.

As a veteran, Steve Rogers is hypercritical when he reflects on his actions on the battlefield. He looks back and takes note of what he could have done differently to save more lives. This is especially true when he thinks of the life of his partner and best friend Bucky. Steve Rogers's need to be hypercritical of his actions in *Captain America: White* can help you better understand you cognitive distortion when using should/shouldn't have statements.

In *Captain America: White* #2, Steve remembers a time when Bucky saved him from drowning. Steve narrates, "I know a little something about holding onto things long after you should. We get attached to these things when it's the people we lost that we should stay attached to. Their hopes and dreams become ours to carry on."[56]

Here, Steve states how someone *should* honor the deceased rather than considering what may be best for one specific person who is mourning the loss of their loved one. When a survivor exhibits the cognitive distortion of should/shouldn't have statements, they think in the same way. Survivors believe events should or should not have been done in a particular manner in a particular situation. They beat themselves up for mistakes they may have made, believing they are not allowed to be human. These thoughts stem from the wrongly-held belief that they could have prevented their sexual abuse if they would have acted differently, and so the abuse was their fault. Overtime, these thoughts impact a survivor's emotions and eventually, their actions. To get rid of these cognitive distortions, it is important to accept that perfection is a myth, even for a super soldier like Steve Rogers. Just as Steve had enhanced abilities but remained imperfect, you will to. Steve needed help and made mistakes the same as anyone else. This is exhibited when Bucky saved him from drowning by stripping Captain America of his excess weight and pulling him to the surface.

Although you may believe that your childhood trauma provided you with heightened abilities to recognize and avoid danger, it is important to remember that everyone makes mistakes, and that healing cannot be accomplished alone. We all need help and support from those we trust. Lean on those closest to you when you find yourself becoming overwhelmed and beginning to drown. Allow them to help pull you back to the surface so you can catch your breath again.

---

56. Loeb, Sale, *Captain America: White.*

Hulk: Gray and All-or-Nothing Thinking

The Incredible Hulk is known for becoming stronger as he gets angrier. In *Hulk: Gray*, Jeph Loeb and Tim Sale present readers with the Hulk's origin story. On the day that would have been his wedding anniversary, Bruce Banner tells his friend, psychiatrist Dr. Leonard Samson, about the first hours of his transformation.

He thinks back to Betty Ross and the beginnings of their relationship. Just as Matt Murdock regrets his inability to save Karen, Bruce regrets his inability to save his fiancée's life. *Hulk: Gray* primarily focuses on Hulk's perception of good and evil through the lens of his relationship with General Thaddeus "Thunderbolt" Ross of the United States Army. This lens demonstrates the cognitive distortion of **all-or-nothing thinking**.

All-or-nothing thinking occurs when events in a survivor's life are viewed in absolute black-and-white categories. This means the survivors believe there can only be right and wrong answers with no gray areas in between. These thoughts lead some survivors to view themselves as being either a hero or a villain. The scene that offers the best understanding of all-or-nothing thinking in *Hulk: Gray* is in issue six when the Hulk and General "Thunderbolt" Ross have a showdown to determine who is the monster and who is the hero.

In this issue, the Hulk rips General Ross out of a crashed helicopter and threatens to kill the General to ensure he is no longer hunted by the United States Army. In the rain and burning debris, Betty asks the Hulk not to kill her father. Ross yells for his daughter to stay out of this confrontation and degrades the Hulk, telling her, "Do you see this creature for what it is?

Or do you still want to play the insolent child?"[57]

In these scenes, Loeb and Sale do an excellent job of depicting similarities between Ross and Hulk. They accomplish this comparison through dialogue and by drawing each man as having one half of the other's face. Although the two are similarly enraged and dogmatic in their views, neither can see their similarities and shared recklessness.

Betty ignores her father and again asks the Hulk not to kill him because she loves him and always will. Upon hearing this plea, the Hulk looks at Betty with an expression of sadness and confusion and says, "Hulk not understand. Hulk not monster. Hulk not hurt Betty. Ross always hurt Betty."[58] Unable to get an answer, the Hulk flings Ross to the ground and jumps away.

Later, the scene in Dr. Sampson's office is drawn in black-and-white, except for Bruce Banner's green eyes. Here, Bruce reflects on that night so many years ago. He tells Leonard with growing anger and self-loathing,

> "Why Betty stayed with me all those years. Even after she found out–after the entire world found out that Bruce Banner is the Hulk. She loved me because she saw the monster as something familiar. As something someone could love. Damn it, Leonard, I've known this all along. I was just too much of a coward to admit it. Me. Ross. What's the difference."[59]

Dr. Sampson attempts to tell his friend that the truth is not

57. Loeb, Sale, *Hulk: Gray.*
58. Loeb, Sale,
59. Loeb, Sale,

so black-and-white, but Bruce sees himself as a perpetrator incapable of love because he saw a reflection of himself in his enemy. The Hulk, Bruce Banner, and General Ross all view themselves, their actions, and the actions of others, in black-and-white terms. No one can be both good and bad. They must be one or the other. There is no gray. Each views themselves and others as being either villains or heroes. Survivors who experience all-or-nothing thinking develop this same view of the world, and themselves in it. This is because as a child, the world could only exist as either black or white. All-or-nothing thinking was the only way to ensure survival.

Judith Herman explains this in her book *Trauma and Recovery* when she states,

> Though [they] perceive [themselves] as abandoned to a power without mercy, [they] must find a way to preserve hope and meaning. The alternative is utter despair, something no child can bear. To preserve [their] faith in [their] parents, [they] must reject the first and most obvious conclusion that something is terribly wrong with them. [They] go to any lengths to construct an explanation for [their] fate that absolves [their] parents of all blame and responsibility.[60]

Judith Herman is explaining how children that have been abused, especially those who have been abused by family members who were supposed to protect them, can develop all-or-nothing thinking as the only way to remain sane. The thought of a loved one (who is supposed to protect them) violating their body in such a traumatic way is unimaginable.

---

60. Herman,

All-or-nothing thinking ensures the child's survival. But later in life, it's a detriment because as an adult, the ability to hold two contradictory truths at once is paramount. The reality in which we live is filled with gray areas. It is not a comic book with identifiable heroes and villains who fit into neat constructs. Instead, it is filled with humans capable of making mistakes. If survivors don't allow for this, they can begin to view themselves and their actions as those of a villain. This mirrors Bruce Banner's belief that the the only reason Betty loved him was because the monster inside him was the same monster he saw inside General Ross. There is no middle ground because he could not see love and joy inside himself.

As a survivor, you may believe those closest to you could never love you if they knew the truths you keep hidden—the Hulk you attempt to keep suppressed. Eliminating the cognitive distortion of all-or-nothing thinking will rid you of the belief that the childhood sexual abuse was your fault. This will allow you to embrace all parts of who you are, and become more intimate with those you love. You do not have to be Bruce Banner, the Hulk, or General Ross. You can be better. You can heal and become the person you were truly meant to be. You can become a survivor.

Spider-Man: Blue and Fortune Telling

Peter Parker and Mary Jane Watson are two names that have become synonymous with Spider-Man. However, it was not Mary Jane Watson, but rather, Gwen Stacey, who was Peter Parker's first love. Unfortunately, Gwen was murdered by the Green Goblin when she was still a teenager, long before she and Peter could begin their life together. In *Spider-Man: Blue*, Peter Parker remembers his relationship with Gwen and attempts to forgive himself for her death. Peter uses a cassette recorder rather than writing letters or speaking to a psychiatrist. Peter's recording demonstrates the cognitive distortion called **fortune telling.**

Fortune telling occurs when survivors arbitrarily attempt to predict the future. Without justification, survivors who fortune-tell assume the worst and/or attempt to will their desired effect into existence. Like mind reading, fortune telling provides survivors with a sense of safety by allowing survivors to feel that they can control their surroundings. Fortune telling lets survivors remain hypervigilant so they can protect themselves from the chaos and loss of control they felt while being sexually abused. In many ways, this cognitive distortion allows survivors to create an imaginary narrative where they can dissociate from reality to survive.

Peter demonstrates fortune telling throughout *Spider-Man: Blue* every time he states a motto that defines the way he views the ups and downs of his life. This begins on the first page of issue one when Peter says to the reader "You see, I've come to believe that things have to get really, really bad before they can get good. Not even really, really good although I wouldn't mind some of that. I guess when you look at the way my life turned out so far, it's about the only way you can look at it. Good follows bad."[61]

Here, Peter reveals that in his personal worldview, things can only get much worse before becoming moderately better. Peter's beliefs about his life offer an example of fortune telling because Peter makes assumptions about negative occurrences

61. Loeb, Sale, *Spider-Man: Blue.*

in his future based solely on bad things that have occurred in his past.

Peter imagines a series of negative situations must occur before his life can improve. Likewise, survivors who fortune tell view the events of their life as a series of defeats that are predestined to occur. Having this view can create a self-fulling prophecy in which the survivor sabotages his own happiness to prove his fortune correct.

Overcoming this distortion means working with a counselor, therapist, or psychiatrist who can help you view events free from labels of "good" or "bad." Instead, you will learn to view an event as something that occurred which cannot be controlled. Sometimes, bad things happen. Other times, good things happen. This is true regardless of an individual's actions or inactions. Life is filled with ups and downs, and none of them should define how we view ourselves. Holding onto the cognitive distortion of fortune telling only fuels a belief that the sexual abuse occurred because we are bad people or that it occurred for unknown religious reasons. Life is unpredictable. All we can do is try our best with what we have been given as we attempt to heal and become better versions of ourselves.

Personalization and Blame of Captain America, Spider-Man, Hulk, and Daredevil

Although Daredevil, Captain America, Hulk, and Spider-Man each have different origin stories, they all share common cognitive distortions of **personalization and blame**. While personalization and blame are two sides of the same coin, each has a different focus. When personalizing, survivors blame themselves for things they were not entirely responsible for, such as a survivor blaming themselves for not getting a promotion at work or losing a difficult competition. On the other hand, blaming places the fault on others while denying the survivor's role in the problem. An example would be blaming others for your inability to control your outburst of rage. Although different, both personalization and blame give survivors a semblance of control. These cognitive distortions also allow survivors to feel righteousness in the false belief that they are completely innocent of all wrongdoing because of the sexual abuse they endured in the past.

Each hero demonstrates their own form of personalization in the different color comics of Jeff Loeb and Tim Sale. For example, in *Captain America: White #1*, Captain America demonstrates both personalization and blame during his first World War II battle. During the battle, a misfire resulted in an explosion that nearly killed Bucky, his teenage sidekick. When the debris settles, Captain America yells at Bucky and says, "One slip-up. One. That's all it takes. And you're going to get yourself killed. I told you it wasn't like the movies."[62] Reflecting back, Captain America thinks to himself, "Maybe I did come down too hard on you that first time or maybe I didn't come down hard enough and you'd still be alive, Bucky."[63]

Both excerpts are excellent examples of how blame and personalization can feed off each other. When a survivor blames others for an incident that went wrong they can immediately personalize the mistake and feel guilty for losing their temper. When this occurs, the survivor regrets having said anything at all and believes the entire incident was their fault from

---

62. Loeb, Sale,
63. Loeb, Sale,

the beginning. Healing means learning to feel your emotions while also not allowing them to control you. This takes time and patience, but it is the only way to accept that the childhood sexual abuse was not your fault.

Peter Parker also demonstrates both personalization and blame in *Spider-Man: Blue* #6 when he states "How many dates—How many kisses did I miss because I was doing this instead of being by your side? I look back on my life as Spider-Man and God help me there are days when all I can think of is how much time it's taken away from my family and everyone I've loved."[64] This excerpt is unique because Peter personalizes his own mistakes and blames his superhero alter ego, Spider-Man, for preventing him from living the life he wishes for with the people he loves.

Peter loves Gwen Stacey and would love to put living his dual identity away to be with her, but the guilt he has over his Uncle Ben's murder forces Peter to feel a responsibility to continue being Spider-Man. Survivors who personalize and blame can behave in a similar manner. They personalize the mistakes of others, believing that others do not have the powers and perspective of life that they developed over time due to the impact of being sexually abused as a child. Then, they take on more responsibility, believing they must do something, rather than wanting to do something. Unfortunately, personalization begins to make them blame the masked personality they show to the world, and this prevents them from being the individual they are keeping hidden away. Without healing, survivors can also begin to blame others for the survivor's need to swoop in and save the day. Examples would be a survivor viewing himself as always having to do the laundry, lend relatives money,

---

64. Loeb, Sale,

or be a listening ear for friends when they have a bad day. The survivor views himself as a savior rather than a human and wishes he was simply allowed to be himself. These survivors need help developing skills to help them communicate better while still establishing and maintaining realistic boundaries.

The Hulk experiences personalization and blame too. These appear in two different excerpts from *Hulk: Gray*. In issue one, Bruce says, "Why does a man who could've used his brain to find a cure for cancer, to find a way to help mankind, build a weapon of mass destruction? Maybe that's why I could never be seen as the hero. Maybe this was the price I had to pay for unleashing the Gamma Bomb into the world."[65]

Later, in the third issue he states, "He was going to let those idiots fire on me. He had heard the reports that bullets would bounce off my—the Hulk's skin and still...with Betty that close...and I was the monster."[66]

In the first excerpt, Bruce personalizes the impact and destruction of the Gamma Bomb, believing his actions are why the Hulk existed and why he could never view himself as the hero. In the second excerpt, Bruce blames General Ross for putting Betty in harm's way. In both instances, Bruce is behaving like a victim rather than a survivor.

In the first comic, Bruce views his intellect as being misused and so views himself as the villain rather than as a human capable of creating both beauty and destruction. In the third comic, Bruce blames Ross for risking Betty's life when Ross orders his men to fire on the Hulk, ignoring the fact that if the Hulk was not present with Betty, she would not have been in harm's way. Both personalization and blame are

65. Loeb, Sale,
66. Loeb, Sale,

forms of viewing yourself as the victim rather than as a survivor. Both are wrong. The goal is to rid yourself of cognitive distortions so you can view incidents as problems where all individuals are neither wholly right nor wholly wrong, but are people who can be held accountable for their actions.

Finally, Daredevil demonstrates personalization in *Daredevil: Yellow* #6 when he states, "All this time I don't think I ever forgave myself for what happened to you. How I've carried around inside me the guilt of knowing that if you hadn't walked into our offices that day, looking for a job, you might be alive today."[67] Here, Daredevil demonstrates how self-forgiveness is difficult. No amount of mind reading or fortune telling can eliminate the impact trauma has on a person, nor can either change the past. In the same way survivors have no way of knowing how their life would have changed if the sexual abuse had not occurred, Matt Murdock has no way of knowing whether Karen would still be alive if she never came to work for the law firm of Nelson and Murdock. It is for this reason personalization can only cause survivors to remain trapped in a cycle of guilt and self-hatred. Daredevil personalizing the death of Karen will not bring her back from the dead, in the same way personalization will not prevent the sexual abuse from occurring in the past. The only way to move forward is to accept that a truly horrific event occurred, not because you did anything wrong, but because you, as a survivor, did not receive the protection and safety you deserved as a child. The sexual abuse was not your fault, but it is your responsibility to heal and break the cycle so you can stop viewing yourself through the lens of a victim and transform into a survivor.

---

67. Loeb, Sale,

Understanding the Childhood Sexual Abuse Was Not My Fault (Autobiographical)

Understanding that the childhood sexual abuse was not my fault was the most difficult path on my journey of healing. For the longest time I believed, beyond the shadow of a doubt, that the sexual abuse was my fault because I was a male and my abuser was a female. I believed that only males could be abusers, and that if I could have prevented myself from having an erection, then none of this would have happened. Working through sessions with my therapist, Susan, I had hit a wall that neither of us could figure out how to traverse. It wasn't until the death of my son, Cas, that I was able to fully accept that the sexual abuse was not my fault. His passing helped me to realize that sometimes, no matter how hard we try, how hyper-vigilant we attempt to be, bad things happen, and they are no one's fault. The journal entry below documents my train of thought and how I came to accept that the childhood sexual abuse I endured from eight to ten years old was not my fault. This journal entry first appeared in my self-help guide *How to Kill Your Batman*.

Losing My Jason Todd (Journal Entry) [68]

For the past two weeks, I've found it difficult to breath due to unknown anxiety and panic. With undue pressure on myself, I've dreaded putting pen to paper or even getting out of bed to go to work. I drifted through the days, sad beyond belief, but smiling, pretending, and performing for family and students to convince myself that everything is fine. Whether because of the

---

68. Rogers, Kenneth

current political climate, problems with my family of origin, or a mixture of both, I couldn't be sure. Either way, I told myself, "I can fix this." What I truly meant was, "I can fix me."

So, I used the tools in my arsenal in an attempt to help myself feel better. I went to the gym, meditated, listened to calming music, went to my therapist (six hours away), went to my psychiatrist (also six hours away), slept, talked with my wife about my feelings (as best I could), [69] and stayed on top of taking my medication. Unfortunately, none of these strategies worked as I would have liked.

One day, near the end of the school day last week, my chest began to hurt, and my left arm became heavy. Sitting at my desk I thought to myself, "No! Not again! I can fix this! I don't need to go to the hospital! I can fix this!" So, I took some ibuprofen (prescribed by my doctor), waited, and the pain went away. I told my therapist, and she said the same thing you're thinking, "You have to go to the hospital. You can't fix this alone." I agreed, but I still have not gone because of fear, stubbornness, and the fact that I've been more times than I care to mention regarding my heart.

You see, two years ago the same incident described above happened. I sat at my desk in my classroom in Baltimore grading papers when my chest began to hurt. I thought it was just another one of my many panic attacks. Soon my left arm went heavy and numb with a pain that's difficult to describe. I could feel my heartrate increase dramatically, and I knew something was not right. I went to the school nurse and soon found myself in an ambulance on my way to the hospital to be treated for a viral heart infection. For two months I went through test after test to understand what, if anything, was wrong with my

---

69. Rogers, Kenneth

heart. I did not enter the classroom, I did not work out, and I could barely move. It was during those two months that I wrote a large portion of *Heroes, Villains, and Healing* (the DC comics edition published in 2017) as quickly as I could out of fear that I might die, and other male survivors would not have the resources needed to heal.

As a male survivor, many times I feel the need to control as much as possible. This is because, as a survivor, my control and power were taken away from me when I was sexually[70] assaulted at eight years old. This is not only true for survivors of sexual assault, but also for many individuals who have suffered trauma or PTSD. Lack of control means lack of power, making the survivor feel as he or she did when sexually assaulted. Hence why Batman attempts to control and plan for all situations. He does not want to feel like that weak little boy on the sidewalk watching his parents die.

I have been told these facts by my therapist for years. I have read them in books, and even written about them myself in *Heroes, Villains, and Healing* and *Raped Black Male*. However, no matter how much I know about the science of the brain and the impact trauma has on the body, I still believe and say to myself, "I can fix this!" because that's what men do, right? We fix things. We identify the problem, form a solution, and get to work. It's what we're told to do as boys to become a part of our hardware as adult men. Add the extra layer of trauma and the belief that men are not supposed to talk about their feelings, and you create anger, fear, panic, anxiety, perpetuation of abuse, domestic violence, gun violence, and suicide. When male survivors think to themselves, "I can fix this!" they are thinking, "I can fix me!" without help. I can pull myself up

---

70. Rogers, Kenneth

by my own bootstraps because that's what "real men" do.

I thought the viral heart infection would teach me differently. I didn't truly learn the lesson that some things can't be fixed until my son, Casus, passed away last August and I nearly lost my wife, Sarah. There were complications with the pregnancy as blood clots formed and attempted to pass. Unfortunately, we lost Cas just as we entered the second trimester. Up until the last moment I believed, "I can fix this!" I thought these same words as my mother cried in my arms when I was in high school, and she received the news that our home was being foreclosed upon. I said these words as a child when my parents would scream at one another late[71] into the night. I believed when the doctors entered the hospital to tell my wife the likelihood of Cas making it was very slim, that I had fixed my life so I could fix this too. I looked Sarah in the eyes and told her we would be fine. We can fix this. We're strong. We can control this. It wasn't until she was wheeled away, and I was left standing in a bathroom of blood that I knew beyond the shadow of a doubt that there was nothing I could do to fix this. I was helpless as our son was born prematurely and died in our arms, my wife was given two blood transfers to save her life, and we signed the paperwork to have him cremated.

I miss Cas. I wear a necklace with the names of him and his two sisters to give me strength when times are hard and I need a reminder of the man I was, the man I have become, and why I'm still breathing. Although I miss my son, he gave me a gift when he passed. With the passing of Cas came the wisdom that horrific things happen, and sometimes there is nothing we can do to stop them. They cannot be fixed, no matter how hard we try, and these bad things are not my fault. They are no one's

---

71. Rogers, Kenneth

fault. Sometimes bad things happen to good people. This does not mean finding something to hate to fill the void of the pain you may feel; it means knowing that it was not your fault.

I now know (most days) that my sexual abuse as a child was not my fault. Bad things happen that are sometimes beyond our control. I was weak then, but that does not mean I am weak now. Many times throughout the week I remind myself of this lesson as my Dark Knight rises and takes hold of my consciousness, refusing to let go. There are some things that cannot be fixed, but there are some things that can be fixed if we ask for help. You are not alone, so don't try and recover alone. Find a way to know and understand that it was not your fault.

PART FOUR

TRANSFORMATION:
Breaking the silence and telling your truth

In *Journey into Mystery #124,* readers discover that Jane Foster is in the hospital after suffering from severe smoke inhalation in the previous issue. Her recovery was supposed to take only a few days, but soon transpired into a prolonged stay. When Don Blake arrives at the hospital, Jane refuses to look in his direction. When Donald Blake asks her why she is acting this way, she tells him, "One moment you're beside me and then you've vanished! I can't bear it anymore! Not knowing where you are—when you'll come back again—or if you'll come back! You've told me you love me—but I know you're keeping some terrible secret from me—some secret you've never allowed me to share!" [72]

With a stern and emotionless face, Donald Blake acknowledges that he wants to tell her the truth but cannot. When Jane

---

72. Lee, Ditko, *Journey into Mystery #124.*

tells him to leave and that she never wants to see him again, Donald Blake slams his walking stick on the floor and transforms into the mighty Thor, revealing to Jane that Donald Blake and Thor are one and the same.

No matter the hero, whether it be Dr. Donald Blake revealing his identity as Thor, billionaire playboy Tony Stark revealing his identity as Iron Man, or quiet and mild-mannered Bruce Banner revealing that he is also the Incredible Hulk, in the land of comic books, truth-telling is difficult, riddled with complications, and invites a host of repercussions. The same is true for survivors, especially male survivors. Societal stigmas portray males as perpetrators of rape and women as victims. For male survivors, the idea of revealing the nature of their sexual abuse to those closest to them often seems impossible, yet telling someone is crucial to a survivor's journey of healing. This chapter explores why you may have remained silent about your childhood sexual abuse for so long, why you should break the silence about your sexual abuse, and how best to disclose the trauma of your childhood sexual abuse to others.

CHAPTER TWELVE

Why You May Have Remained Silent

Although Donald Blake does not reveal his identity as Thor to Jane Foster until *Journey into Mystery #124*, in *Journey into Mystery #90*, Donald Blake makes the decision to tell Jane that he loves her and reveal his identity as Thor. He is stopped when his father Odin appears to him and states, "Heed my words, Lord of Thunder! You are bound never to reveal your identity to any other mortal! I have spoken!" [73] Because of Odin's warning, Donald Blake takes much longer to reveal his dual identity to Jane. When he does, Odin vows to make Thor pay for going against his wishes by telling Jane his secret identity.

When Thor returns to Asgard in *Journey into Mystery #124*, Odin decides to hold a Ritual of Steel wherein his son will be killed by the warriors of Asgard, men who were once Thor's brothers in arms. Should Thor survive, Odin plans to

---

73. Lieber, Lee, Hartley, *Journey into Mystery #90*.

imprison him on Asgard to prevent him from venturing to Earth. Odin's reaction to Thor's truth-telling is a great metaphor for why so many survivors refrain from revealing the nature of their childhood sexual abuse to others. The fear of telling is often less about the survivor's apprehension, and more about facing a negative response from other people. When Donald Blake revealed his secret to Jane, he was apprehensive and nervous, but not enough to stop him; he knew telling her was the right thing to do. However, the impact his truth telling would have on his father kept him silent. Similar to Thor, survivors of sexual abuse may feel conflicted about disclosing their childhood sexual abuse to others, but the real fear is telling may cause a fallout with family and friends. Survivors fear that these people may suddenly turn against them, the same way Thor's comrades were willing to fight him to death for breaking Odin's orders.

As a child, you may have wanted to tell someone about your sexual abuse. You may have even told others and not been believed. You may have been told, "that's impossible," "that can't happen to boys," or "that's a girl thing." Unfortunately, this may also happen as an adult. Some adult males may praise the sexual abuse if it came at the hand of an attractive female, claiming, "now you're a man" or "it will make you a beast at it later."

Furthermore, sexual abuse of boys is often hidden from the public because there's a belief that the abuse will somehow reflect negatively on the family, even if the perpetrator was not a family member. When the perpetrator is a neighbor, coach, or close friend of the family, the sexual abuse is still not reported as often as it is when a girl is sexually abused by the same individuals. The family may believe they are protecting the boy by not bringing attention to the abuse. They may think they are preventing a negative backlash in the form of bullying and homophobic comments. Although they may think they are protecting the child, by not talking about the abuse, they send the message that what happened to the boy is unimportant, that he is unimportant, and that he must suffer his trauma in silence.

If the sexual abuse was incestuous and occurred at the hands of an aunt, uncle, cousin, sister, brother, mother, or father, there is a pervasive belief that it should be handled by the family so as not to "air dirty laundry." The image of the family is placed before the needs of the boy who was sexually offended. Sometimes, the sexual abuse is simply not believed. Either circumstance ostracizes the male survivor, leaving the abused person feeling alone and without value, as though their emotions are not important because they are not important. The survivor will often stop trusting family members to do what is right rather than what is easy.

Stifling the voices of sexually abused boys forces the men they become to live a dual life behind their secret identity, or to live as a stoic man who suppresses their emotions. Instead of receiving support from other males in their life such as their fathers, uncles, cousins, and grandfathers, male survivors are conditioned to remain silent. Like Thor, who was forced to remain silent by his father, they push down their emotions, continue to fight through any hardship until it is defeated, and self-medicate through drugs and alcohol if the pain becomes too much to bear. It is a vicious cycle that only ends when it is broken.

The final reason survivors may not disclose their childhood sexual abuse is that they are afraid it will change the way others view them. Speaking of childhood trauma gives others a glimpse into a person at his most vulnerable. Rather than others viewing him as a superhero god who has it all together, they may view him as a weak and crippled man unable to take care of himself.

You may feel as though others can see directly through you, exposing you completely to the world. Disclosure requires a leap of faith and trust in others that you were not prepared to have before beginning your journey of healing. This may make you feel as though you are giving up the last semblance of control you have over your childhood sexual abuse, because before you disclose your truth, you retain complete control of who knows this secret and who does not. You may feel this control is all the power you have left. Although you may fear relinquishing this control, speaking and disclosing your sexual abuse will provide you with a wealth of strength you may not have known you had.

Civil War and Why You Should or Should Not Disclose

Marvel Comic's 2006-2007 *Civil War Saga* is all about truth, identity, and legality versus reality. In this series, the United States government has passed a law that requires all superheroes to sign a registry and reveal their true identity to the government. Anyone caught resisting will spend the rest of their life in prison. At the saga's conclusion, the dynamics of the Marvel Universe change forever. The superhero community is split down the middle. Some, such as Mr. Fantastic and She-Hulk, believe having superheroes reveal their identity serves the greater good of society. Others, such as Captain America and Falcon, believe that forcing a superhero to reveal their identity places the superhero, and all those they love, in danger. As a result, some heroes go into hiding to protect their anonymity while others, such as Iron Man, hold press conferences to reveal their secret identity to the world.

In *Civil War: Frontline #1,* Tony Stark makes the choice to reveal his identity as Iron Man to the world. While this may not have been the right choice for other superheroes, it was Tony's choice, made on his own without coercion. It is for this reason and this reason alone that it was the right choice for him. Tony knew that revealing himself to be Iron Man would not put anyone he loved in danger because he did not have a family to protect; he only had himself. Unlike with Thor, there was no decree from on high stating he could not tell the world who he was. There was only the code he had made for himself as a hero, and that could be changed whenever and however he saw fit.

While Tony's revelation to the world worked out well for him, the same cannot be said for Peter Parker. In *Civil War: Frontline #2,* Peter Parker holds a similar press conference in which he unmasks and reveals to the world that he is the friendly neighborhood Spider-Man. Unlike Tony, Peter did not make the decision to disclose his identity on his own. He was coerced to reveal his Spider-Man identity by his wife Mary Jane Watson, Tony Stark, and his Aunt May. Against his better judgement and his personal code as a hero, Peter disclosed the truth of his identity. The results are much different for him than they were for Tony Stark. The world praised Tony for his bravery, and Stark Enterprise's stock increased in value when the government contracted him with the task of imprisoning heroes who refused to disclose their identity. Meanwhile, the world grew to hate Peter, transforming the perception of his actions from those of a hero to those of a villain.

Although Tony promised Peter that he would protect Mary

Jane and Aunt May from harm, all that changed when Peter realized he was on the right side of the law but the wrong side of morality. Peter realized there is a difference between doing what is right and following the law. After publicly stating that superheroes were being imprisoned into inhumane circumstances, and siding with Captain America against the superhero registration act, a sniper shot Aunt May, and Peter Parker and Mary Jane had to run from the law while trying to pay Aunt May's medical expenses out of pocket. Eventually, Spider-Man's enemies smelled the blood in the water and the superhero's life was turned upside down.

Tony Stark's and Peter Parker's stories correspond to how difficult it is for a survivor to disclose the nature of their childhood sexual abuse. Peter's disclosure of his superhero identity suggests that survivors should not disclose the nature of their childhood sexual abuse until they are certain they are ready. Peter was not ready to tell the world that he was Spider-Man. He felt pressured by his boss, wife, and surrogate mother to ignore his intuition and discard his superhero code, and because he ignored his intuition, no good came from his disclosure.

Only the survivor should make the choice to disclose. While it is important for survivors to discuss their sexual abuse as a child with a spouse or partner to prepare them for possible reactions during sex, they should only do so when they feel safe and comfortable. This means it's crucial to ensure there is a strong foundation of support. If speaking of the sexual abuse feels uncomfortable, or you feel extreme distress, you should stop, discuss the feelings and thoughts with a counselor or therapist, and continue to build a supportive foundation before continuing.

Tony's disclosure of his identity mirrors how breaking the

silence can also mean breaking the cycle of abuse. Tony primarily acts as a villain throughout much of the *Civil War Saga*, yet his disclosure likely provided others with the courage to reveal their superhero identities to their loved ones. Male survivors who hear the testimony of other survivors may also discover the strength needed to disclose their sexual abuse when they realize they are not alone in their trauma.

Publicly disclosing your childhood sexual abuse to those other than relatives and loved ones is not for everyone. Revealing the nature of your abuse to so many people creates a bigger likelihood that at least one of those people might be someone who enjoys causing others pain. This is especially true for male survivors since the belief that men and boys cannot be sexually abused or assaulted is still pervasive. People who think that way may believe you are seeking attention, or are no longer a real man when you tell the truth of your sexual abuse. These negative statements and backward beliefs can cause setbacks in your journey of healing, especially if you are not yet prepared to live comfortably in your truth. However, telling your story informs others who have and have not been sexually abused that male sexual abuse does and can occur. It also informs others that this form of sexual abuse and assault is not uncommon. Speaking gives voice to the voiceless and provides strength where it was taken away.

Another reason to speak out about your sexual abuse is to take control over a part of your life that was taken away. When Tony removes his helmet in *Civil War: Frontline #1,* he does not reveal his identity in the same cinematic way he does in the movies. Instead of boldly stating that he is Iron Man, he says "Hello. My name is Tony Stark, and I am an alcoholic. And now it's time to come clean." [74] Just as acknowledging his addiction to alcohol in *Iron Man #128* "Demon in a Bottle" provided him the strength to regain control of a situation that was spiraling out of control, revealing his identity allowed him to feel free to be his complete self all the time, rather than having to hide behind a mask.

Over time, as you learn to identify as a survivor, you will become proud of the man you have become. Speaking sheds light on the past and stops it from being frightening. It gives the abuse shape and substance, and allows it to be seen, addressed, so you can be healed. Learning to disclose sexual abuse to others takes time, practice, and guidance by a counselor or therapist. In the beginning, it will not be easy. You'll make mistakes and shed tears as you become the most vulnerable you have ever been, but it will become easier, and you will be stronger and better for it.

74. Jenkins, Watson, *Civil War: Front Line #1*.

CHAPTER THIRTEEN

How to Disclose Your Childhood Sexual Abuse

Speaking and discussing your childhood sexual abuse with a trained counselor or therapist does not require preparation. A professional will have been trained to address and discuss sexual abuse in a way that allows you to feel comfortable and safe. However, disclosing sexual abuse to close friends or family does require preparation. Analyzing how heroes disclose their truths can help survivors decide how to progress through the different stages of disclosing their sexual abuse.

Lack of Emotion

In *The Amazing Spider-Man* #87 "Unmasked at Last," Peter believes he is losing his abilities as Spider-Man and, as a result, he reveals his identity. The comic begins with Peter analyzing a sample of his blood to determine why he feels so weak, has a fever, is experiencing chills, has been having dizzy spells, and is hallucinating. When he is unable to find answers of his own and he cannot locate Doctor Connors, Peter believes he only has a few hours before he loses his Spider-Man abilities completely. He decides the only logical decision is to come clean to his friends about his secret identity. Peter arrives at his girlfriend Gwen Stacey's birthday party in normal clothes, but he has his Spider-Man mask in hand. He tells Gwen, her father, Harry Osbourne, and Mary Jane, "Spider-Man is finished! His career is ended forever! I'm the only one who could know that because I'm Spider-Man!" [75]

Peter's words are written in exclamation marks but his expression and demeanor are anything but excited. Instead, he looks shocked and confused. Sweat drips down his face and there are more thought bubbles than actual words as Peter apologizes and runs into the night. Shortly after, Peter goes to an emergency room and discovers that he simply has the flu. He convinces everyone that he was having a hallucination and has someone else dressed as Spider-Man appear in the window as a viable alibi.

The expression on Peter's face and the way he reveals his identity reflect the way many survivors may look and feel the first time they reveal their childhood sexual abuse to those they love. When disclosing the nature of childhood sexual abuse, the survivor often retells the nature of their abuse with a **lack of emotion or feeling**. The past is recounted as if the sexual abuse happened to someone else or as if it were a scene in a movie. Rather than yell hysterically as they come to terms with their traumatic past, many survivors reveal the nature of their childhood trauma numbly, as if they are in a daze. They are unsure of what exactly to say, and they don't know how

---

75. Lee, Romita Sr., *The Amazing Spider-Man #87*.

others will react, so they speak of their childhood sexual abuse as if it happened to someone else. This is common, although survivors can also disclose their abuse in the opposite manner too.

Childish

In *The Amazing Spider-Man* #200 "The Spider and the Burglar," Peter Parker confronts the man who killed his uncle, Ben Parker, when the villain escapes from prison and returns to the Parker's home in an attempt to find money that he stashed away there decades prior. When Peter realizes the nameless killer has returned, he is filled with rage and searches for the man to make him pay for what he has done.

In an abandoned warehouse, Spider-Man finds his uncle's killer. The villain is confused about why Spider-Man is pursuing him so vehemently. He doesn't understand why Spider-Man is so concerned about the safety of the Parkers, in particular. In reaction to the villain's confusion, Peter rips off his mask and reveals a face full of hatred when he states "You really wanna know, creep? All right—take a look! I care because Ben Parker was my uncle!" [76] When the villain sees Peter Parker's face beneath the Spider-Man mask, he realizes Peter will never stop seeking revenge on him until one them is dead.

When Peter discloses his identity in anger, he is demonstrating the second way in which many survivors reveal their childhood sexual abuse. Rather than explain the nature of their abuse with a lack of emotion, some survivors do it in a way that is in an abundance of unbridled emotion. This is what it

---

76. Lee, Wolfman, Pollard, *The Amazing Spider-Man* #200.

means to reveals your abuse in a childish manner. This means the sexual abuse is disclosed in the manner of a child who has been hurt. The survivor discloses his abuse to gain sympathy and tears. He may relive the abuse for the first time. In "The Spider and the Burglar," Peter wants to frighten his uncle's killer in the same way that some survivors want to confront their abuser. This mirrors how a child often wants to hurt the individual who hurt them.

The only way to achieve a healthy disclosure of your childhood sexual abuse is to continue to disclose it until you find yourself in the final stages of disclosure—truth telling. Mary Jane Watson embodies this healthy type of disclosure when she reveals the nature of her traumatic childhood to Peter Parker and reveals that she has known he is Spider-Man for a long time.

Truth

When a survivor discloses the nature of their childhood sexual abuse **truthfully,** the survivor acknowledges the effects the abuse had on the survivor's life as a child and as an adult. Furthermore, truth means the survivor knows and accepts that there was nothing that they could have done to prevent the abuse. The individual knows they are a survivor of childhood sexual abuse and identifies with that part of themselves rather than pushing that part away. Mary Jane Watson displays this level of truth-telling in *The Amazing Spider-Man* #259 "All My Past Remembered" when she reveals that she knows Peter Parker is Spider-Man, and she speaks her truths about her traumatic past and why it was time for her to heal.

In this comic, Mary Jane reveals that she grew up in an

abusive home. As she and Peter walk through Central Park, she tells Peter about her mother and father. Her father was a struggling writer who forced the family to move from university to university throughout his career as a professor. He would often take out his frustrations on Mary Jane's mother and sometimes on Mary Jane and her older sister, Gayle.

Mary Jane and her family went to live with their cousin, Frank Brown, to escape the father's abuse. Frank allowed them to move in, providing that Mary Jane's mother would take care of him and his children since his wife had died a year earlier. The Watsons went from one abusive situation to another as Gayle followed in her mother's footsteps.

Mary Jane watched Gayle marry and begin a family with a man who did not want to be a husband or a father. When Gayle became pregnant for the second time, her husband abandoned them. Then Mary Jane's mother passed away from illness. Through each circumstance, Mary Jane explains how she coped with the trauma by being the center of attention and putting on a façade of perpetual happiness. She tells how she would flirt and end relationships without explanation rather than commit to any relationship. She never allowed anyone to get too close for too long because she was afraid of becoming like her mother or sister. She could not take the risk of reliving the same cycle and giving up on her dreams for someone else. As a result of these fears, Mary Jane ran out on her sister when their mother passed away.

She did not want the responsibility of caring for a family she did not choose. Occasionally, while revealing these truths, she cries. Sometimes she looks at Peter, and other times she is reflective, and her focus is elsewhere. She does not tell Peter the details of her traumatic past to gain his love or to make him feel sorry for her. She reveals her past because she trusts Peter with the truth. She lets Peter see who she is behind the façade to grow closer to him, and to show Peter that true intimacy is a two-way street. Mary Jane knows Peter Parker is Spider-Man, and Peter knows Mary Jane Watson is not the happy-go-lucky flake he believed her to be. Both know the other is human, flawed, and that beneath the masks they wear, there is a vulnerable person capable and deserving of love.

This is what it means for survivors to disclose their childhood sexual abuse with truthfulness. Truth-telling should not be a spectacle like it was for Tony Stark and Peter Parker when they held press conferences to reveal their true identities. As a public figure in the limelight, this form of truth telling was reflective of Tony's personality. As a survivor, when you tell your story, it should be intimate and feeling, but there should not be an overwhelming outburst of emotion, whether that be anger or sadness. There is only the honesty that something bad happened to you in the past; you are healing from it; and it does not define who you are as an individual. This is what it means to become a survivor and overcomer.

Progressing toward truth-telling requires practice, patience, and grace with yourself as you make mistakes. In the beginning, you'll feel vulnerable. However, in time, your disclosures will become less difficult and more comfortable.

It is also important to know there are many ways to disclose the nature of your sexual abuse. You can express your experiences through art, dance, writing, or speaking. Explore what feels most comfortable, and progress through this stage with the needed support of those around you.

As an example of how disclosure can take many different forms, I've included a short story I wrote which expressed the nature of my sexual abuse long before I ever began my journey of healing. It was first published in 2007 in my book of short stories, *Thoughts in Italics*.

Action Guy (Fiction)

This is my room. I got toys! I got lots of toys! Not as many as before, but I still got toys. And they're not as new as they used to be. This one's broken, but that's okay. I still like it without the siren. I don't need a siren as long as it still rolls. I can make the siren noise. See? *Wrrr!* Got to put out the fire! Hurry! *Wrrr!* See? It still works. Even without the siren. I got other toys though. I got a sailboat, a wagon, and…Oh! Action Guy! I love Action Guy! He can do everything. Fly. *Swwiisshh!* Beat up bad guys. *Bang! Pow!* Burst through walls. *Boom!* And go wherever he wants by just thinking it. I wish I had that power. Just close my eyes really tight, think really hard about some place far away and, *poof*, I'm there. Anywhere! On a mountain, in the sky, in China, anywhere! That would be so cool. To go outside.

I used to go places like Action Guy. Run in the grass and stuff, play, but not anymore. Not with the door locked. The door is always locked, at least now. It wasn't before. Before the bad thing. Before…before the walls used to be blue, bright blue. And I had lots of toys. New toys with sounds, and lights, and cool, bright colors. There was a carpet, and outside my windows I could see clouds and sky and grass and sun. It was fun! But now…now it's different since the bad thing. I'm not supposed to talk about the bad thing. It's not like it used to be since it happened. The walls are dirty and faded. The carpet is gone, and the wood is hard and cold and creaks when I walk on it. And the clouds are gone. The windows are bricked up, and I only have one tiny little hole to look out of. And I can't see anything through it. Only sun. One small dot of sun. My toys are old and no one comes to see me. I'm always the only person here. I like to play by myself, but sometimes…sometimes I wish I had someone else to make the siren noise and I don't always have to make believe to be happy.

No one ever let me out after the bad thing. After she made me do stuff I didn't wanna do. I didn't want to play that game anyway. She made me! She said it would be fun! It wasn't fun! It was never fun. It was scary and made me feel bad. She made me touch…and…and to get on top of her. I didn't want to. I never wanted to. But I did. So, I got in trouble. I got locked in here for being bad. It's my fault. I shouldn't have done it. Now I'm being punished. No more toys, no more clouds, or sun, or fun stuff. It's all my fault. Now I'm being punished. Now I have to wait for someone to unlock the door. They'll come. I know they will. Action Guy will come and break down the door, kick out the bricks in the windows, and then he'll grab my hand and we'll squeeze our eyes together really tight like this, and then, *poof*, we'll be outside in the sun. Flying all day and won't be my fault no more and the bad thing will be over. But—but the door is still locked and Action Guy hasn't come yet, so I guess— I guess I'll wait and play by myself. Like I always do.[77]

Writing Exercise #7: Revealing Your Secret Identity

Depending on where you are on your journey through the healing process, you may or may not have the ability to complete this writing exercise.

Every superhero has an identity they feel must be kept secret to protect themselves and those closest to them. Many

---

77. Rogers Jr., *Thoughts in Italics,*

survivors of childhood sexual abuse also appeal to secrecy as a form of strength. This may be why they are commonly drawn to heroes in the first place. Unfortunately, the real world is not a comic book, and secrets only give strength to perpetrators and abusers. True strength comes from taking back control by disclosing childhood sexual abuse and shedding light on past trauma. Talking creates knowledge, awareness, support, and trust where you previously believed there was none.

If you have decided to regain control and become strong enough to disclose the nature of your childhood sexual abuse to anyone, reflect on the experience. How did you react? How did you feel? If you have not told anyone about the nature of your sexual abuse as a child, it may be beneficial to write what you believe their reaction may be. Journal about how you felt to help you prepare to be fully intimate with those you care for as you rid yourself of the old façade.

The next chapter is a full recounting of my journey throughout this stage of the healing process. The story spans over twenty years of my life and reveals why it took me so long to tell the truth about my childhood sexual abuse.

CHAPTER FOURTEEN

My Truth-Telling (Autobiographical)

At eight years old, I was sexually abused by my older sister. For two years, I was forced to have sex with her while watching pornographic movies. The abuse abruptly came to an end because my sister either realized it was wrong or feared becoming pregnant. Maybe it was a combination of both. It wasn't until years later that she disclosed that she had been sexually abused when she was eight years old by her babysitter, Mr. Miller. This is not to excuse her of her actions, but to allow understanding of her attempts to cope with her childhood sexual abuse.

I didn't reach a point in my life where I could say and write these words without an overwhelming feeling of shame and guilt until twenty-five years later, after years of therapy, and full disclosure of my abuse to the members of my family.

While growing up, I was afraid to even think about being raped. I wasn't even aware it was wrong until I said to a group of friends in elementary school that I had sex with my sister, and they found it disgusting. Incest was not a word I had learned. Once the definition of the word was clear to me, I began to battle with the question of whether or not I was still a virgin. Did my abuse qualify as legitimate sex? Was it supposed to be cool or disgusting to have lost my virginity at such a young age? Was I eternally damned to hell for losing my virginity at such a young age without being married?

As these questions bounced from one to the other throughout my head, I fell into myself, reading and writing in my journals whenever possible. Even with each question about life, death, and hopeless romanticism, I dared not write about the sexual abuse out of fear that someone might read the journal and I would "get in trouble."

Domestic abuse and arguments between my parents throughout high school left me and my mother homeless during my junior and senior year. We lived in the basements of cousins, uncles, and aunts. Attempting to handle this trauma pushed the sexual abuse of my childhood further from my thoughts as I battled depression, anxiety, and simply making it day-to-day.

Throughout these years, it never crossed my mind that my sexual abuse as a child could also have been a factor in my feelings of isolation and loneliness. To fight these emotions as best I could, I participated in any and all extracurricular activities and overachieved in academics. These tactics became my primary means of coping with, rather than disclosing, my sexual abuse.

College offered a new chapter. The possibility of denying that I had been raped at eight years old became nearly impossible with the introduction to having sexual partners. The lies my brain was able to create to deny my sexual abuse were revealed through my body in the form of uncontrollable shaking following each sexual encounter with a new partner. It was here that I first disclosed the sexual abuse of my childhood to a few of my sexual partners. There weren't many. I quickly learned that for me, one-night stands were not an option.

However, I cared for the few partners I had and felt it was my responsibility to let them know my physical reactions had nothing to do with them, but were the result of traumatic events from my past. Although I told myself I was disclosing my sexual abuse for them, I was actually doing it for myself. I was seeking sympathy and a savior to relieve the pain I had been harboring for years. I lay in their arms, shaking and expecting all the pain and anxiety of the past to wash away with each uttered syllable. I wonder if other survivors also seek this form of savior and safety in the people they love? Unfortunately, each time I disclosed my feelings of isolation and loneliness in this childish manner, the outcome remained the same.

It was not until years later, after the birth of my eldest daughter, Mirus, that I entered the Emergency Stage and began the process of healing. Following a year of therapy and medication, I felt I was ready to begin the process of truthfully disclosing the nature of my sexual abuse.

Telling Aunt Margaret

My wife, Sarah, had already known for years about my sexual abuse, but rather than telling my own parents, the first person I told beyond my wife was my wife's aunt, Margaret. In my head I had rehearsed what I was going to say and how I would say it. I promised myself there would be no tears. It would be explained as a matter of fact. Truth. Nothing more, nothing less.

The reason I chose Aunt Margaret as the first person to tell was that she was, and still is, a person I can trust and not have to explain my emotions to. This is a quality my wife inherited, and it's one of the primary reasons I fell in love with her. I remember telling Aunt Margaret facts about my abuse somewhat unemotionally, as I searched for kindness and sympathy from her. She expressed her regret, sadness, support, and praise for my courage, which I accepted. In this way, my disclosure was like a child seeking sympathy from an adult for the wrongs of the world, but in many ways, this is what I needed. I needed someone other than Sarah or my therapist Susan, to express regret for my childhood trauma. To remind me that what I had experienced was difficult but hadn't broken me. Not completely. I was a good man who strived to do the right thing and that made all the difference. It gave me the courage to continue to tell my truth.

From there I told my family, beginning with my sister. Although she was the abuser, she deserved to know that others in the family would know about an incident that affected her as well. Rather than make a phone call I was unsure I could handle, and because we had stopped talking when I had begun therapy, I sent her a text message letting her know I was going to tell the family about what had happened between us as kids. I also invited her to a therapy session with me, but she declined. She was not ready to begin her journey of healing. I'm still not sure if she is.

Telling Daniel

Next, I told my brother, Daniel. Throughout my first year of therapy, I struggled through my Emergency Stage. All that time, Daniel had been my primary cheerleader. None of that changed after I disclosed my sexual abuse. After I told him our sister was the perpetrator, he believed he was partly to blame because conflicts between him and my father had led him to leave the house and join the military. I assured him there was nothing he could have done, and that he was the only one who had nothing to be held accountable for. Unfortunately, he had to work to accept that the abuse was not his fault in the same way I had to work through that stage on my journey of healing.

During this conversation, I began to feel more comfortable telling my truth. The story brought forward more of my emotions, but I was still able to tell it truthfully. I did not have tears nor anger, and I was not searching for pity or sadness, which let me know I was not telling my story childishly or numbly. Instead, I was speaking in a way that shared my story with someone I cared for. I wanted family, and with Daniel I didn't feel so alone. I still don't. He's my best friend.

Telling My Mother

Third, I told my mother. I knew she would be the most difficult person to tell. Although I would have preferred to tell her in person, I could not because of the distance between Peoria, Illinois and Baltimore, Maryland. I could not afford to drive twelve hours to visit, tell her, and drive back in a single weekend. Instead, I called her on the phone.

The conversation began with me reassuring her that I was fine and getting help, but that she should know I had been raped by my sister (her daughter) for two years, beginning when I was eight years old. She said very little, apologized, and seemed to get off the phone relatively quickly.

At the time, I felt a little hurt that she didn't say more, but months later she explained that she had felt shocked and ashamed that this had happened in her house, and she had no idea. The other reason for her silence was that my sister had already told her about the sexual abuse years before but had told her the sexual abuse had only happened once. The truth of what had actually happened left her reeling. To help us both heal from this trauma, she came to Baltimore, attended a book signing and discussion of my book, *Raped Black Male*, came to a joint therapy session to better understand why the abuse occurred, and sincerely apologized for this ever happening to me. Over the years, she has continued to remain supportive.

Telling My Father

Finally, I told my father. This was a conversation I did not know how to prepare for, so I began in the same way I had with my mother. I reassured him that I was OK, but that for two years I had been raped by my sister (his daughter). Although the conversation began in the same way, it ended much differently. After explaining the sexual abuse, he said to me, "Forget about it. It's in the past. The best thing you can do is move on."

To say I was shocked at his response would be an understatement. However, I found that I was not only shocked, but angry as well. Rather than cower and continue to harbor the secret I had been carrying for over twenty years, I responded with defiance and honesty. I told him that I couldn't forget. The abuse was something I had to live with every day and that it could not be forgotten. He apologized, hung up, and did not speak with me for nine months. It wasn't until Daniel told him that he needed to start talking to me that my father proceeded to begin texting and speaking with me as if nothing had happened. The illusion of normalcy was not something I could return to, so (under the instruction of my therapist) I asked my father for a written letter apologizing for abandoning me after I told him about the sexual abuse. Rather than comply, he responded back via text. He said:

> *Okay, son. I will respect your request. You are a grown man and able to make your own decisions. I'm glad you are doing better and I'm really sorry to hear about Sarah's brother. Let me say this...I love my kids the same. You, Daniel, and (my sister) are my life. I don't love one more or less than the other one. If I could take your hurt I would. I can't so I can do only what I am able to do. But remember this. We can only start healing after we forgive. If I could change things I would. I'm sure your sister is hurting. I'm sure she had no intention of hurting you. Then or now. She has to live with the fact of what she did and face everyone who read your book and label her a rapist. This has to be really hard for her. I'm sure this has been really hard on you. I can only imagine how hard it has been. I know my kid and know you are strong. You can and will overcome this. It's in the blood. No matter what you think, this too will pass. If you need me I will always be there for you. Don't be a stranger. I don't want you to one day think I missed out on a lot of my family's life. She, Daniel, Tina and me are your family. Love you unconditionally. Da.*

It's taken a long time to digest these words and understand

them. The message does a number of things. First, it minimized my sexual abuse and sympathizes with the abuser rather than the victim. When he said, "She has to live with the fact of what she did and face everyone who read your book and label her a rapist," he reveals a need to not "air dirty laundry" and hold people accountable for their actions by using the correct language to describe their behavior. A person who forces an individual to have sex against their will is a rapist. There is no doubt the word causes pain to the individual being labeled as such, but there is no other word to describe those actions. It is regrettable to have to use this word in reference to my sister, but to do otherwise would be to not hold the abuser accountable. That also fails to attempt to stop the cycle of sexual abuse.

Second, the message reveals my father's refusal to take responsibility for his failure as a parent to protect his children. Although he says, "If I could take your hurt I would," this statement and others do not reveal his knowledge or acceptance of his role in allowing this to happen. A parent's responsibility is to protect their children. To not do so does not mean the parent has failed because there is no such thing as the perfect parent. Mistakes will be made. However, following those mistakes, parents must admit their shortcomings to let their children know that what happened was not the child's fault and so the parent can apply what they have learned to future situations. Unfortunately, my father does not accept any accountability and so places the blame on the shoulders of others.

Third, it reveals the mentality of many men, especially black men, who came of age before and during the Civil Rights Movement. My father makes statements such as, "I know my kid and I know you are strong," and "It's in the blood." These statements are similar to Norman Osbourn's statements to his son, Harry, when he tells him to be more of a man and not be so soft. My father's words are similar because they reveal a need to teach boys to remain silent and unfeeling, and to deny pain and move on from life's hardships. For older black men, this mentality was important because during the Civil Rights Movement and the era of Jim Crow, denial of pain, hardships, and abuse was the only way to survive. It was their coping mechanism to handle physical abuse and the mental trauma of not being able to keep their family safe. Denying hurt could have prevented men like my father from being lynched and killed since he grew in rural Mississippi. Denial and forgetting were the only coping strategies fathers could pass on to their sons when basic human rights had been stripped away. This means that when their sons, nephews, and cousins suffered a traumatic episode, such as childhood sexual abuse, they taught and reinforced the only way of life they have ever known, which is to forget it ever happened and bury the emotions that accompany trauma. This is not a justification for his message about my sexual abuse, but it provides context for my understanding of why he said what he said. As a male survivor, understanding means no longer viewing myself as a victim, understanding the wrongs of the past, learning from them, and moving forward.

Following my disclosure of my childhood sexual abuse to my immediate family, I told my in-laws, close friends, and extended family. With each disclosure I felt more empowered and encouraged to help male survivors like myself. This empowerment and urge to help is why I wrote *Raped Black Male*. It's why I continue to write and speak—to continue along my journey of healing and to help others along theirs. Speaking my truth has taught me about intimacy and trust, and that silence is not an option.

PART FIVE

MASTER OF TWO WORLDS:
Resolution, moving on, and post-traumatic growth

Why do we love and idolize superheroes? Is it their super abilities that leave us captivated and awestruck? Or is it the definitive example of good versus evil that appeals to us? There could be any number of reasons circulating through the "What If" multi-verse.

Although our individual appreciation of superheroes and villains varies, as a male survivor, I am inclined to believe the obsession stems from the possibility of transformation and the belief that someone can dramatically change into something new, different, and better.

Will Booker explores the appeal for transformation offered by comics in the essay "We Could Be Heroes" in the book *What is a Superhero?* when he states, "The best heroes are those with hidden, hurt, and secret wounds—ones who channel some of their creators' outsider status and reflect back some of their reader's insecurity." [78] He explores the notion that we view versions of ourselves in the heroes we idolize, and that we can see our pain and trauma reflected back to us in the superheroes we read about on the page and watch on the silver screen. He goes on to state, "Superhero mythology is about escape, about creating an alternative identity and becoming someone different, someone better." [79] In essence, we need these heroes as models for becoming better versions of ourselves.

When venturing into the world of comics we are looking for escape and the possibility of improvement. The possibility of growth and transformation embodied by superheroes mirrors what healing offers to survivors. Progressing along the journey of healing, after Crossing the First Threshold, marching along the Road of Trials, and achieving self-forgiveness through Atonement, you'll become the Master of Two Worlds.

This colossal transformation into something better and different occurs for all superheroes after acquiring their superpowered abilities. There is the moment of traumatic impact when the average individual is bestowed extraordinary abilities following a tragic accident. Bruce Banner's ability to transform into the Hulk followed his exposure to a detonated gamma-radiation bomb; Peter Parker's abilities as Spider-Man came after he was bitten by a radioactive spider; and for the Fantastic Four, abilities materialized after they were bombarded with a wave of cosmic radiation in outer space. The list of ordinary characters and how they developed their super abilities is exhaustive, extending from the depths of space with Norrin Radd as the Silver Surfer, to transformations on

78. Booker, *What is a Superhero?*
79. Booker,

Earth when Luke Cage becomes a Hero for Hire. Although these transformations are appealing, they are not realistic examples of the transformation process as experienced by everyday individuals in this reality, nor does their immediacy represent the continuous journey of healing for survivors.

In comics, following a few moments of initial pain, a new character is born. After a few colorful pages of trial, error, and minimal conflict, the superhero becomes the Master of Two Worlds. He is easily able to move freely from one plane of existence to another. Of course, there are occasionally hiccups along the way, but usually, the two worlds the superhero occupies remain separate. Rarely do they integrate. Instead, the hero works to maintain the balance of two separate systems, actively preventing one from bleeding into the other.

This is not the balance meant to be achieved when striving to become the master of two worlds. The process described above is not realistic. Rarely do comic books properly depict the transformation of a character who develops a different outlook on life from what they had prior to the accident. However, there is one series that provides a great context to understand the difficult transformative process survivors often undergo when venturing along the path of healing. This series involves the Man Without Fear.

CHAPTER FIFTEEN

Daredevil and Becoming the Master of Two Worlds

In the six-part series, *Daredevil: Born Again,* the King Pin of crime, Wilson Fisk, discovers the secret identity of Daredevil. This happens when Karen Page, Matt Murdock's love interest and former secretary of Nelson and Murdock, sells his identifying information in exchange for drugs. King Pin does not take the information to locate and kill Matt Murdock; instead, the villain uses the information to ruin Matt's life and reputation.

Fisk calls in favors to have Matt Murdock fired from his job, audited by the I.R.S., and disbarred from practicing law when a police officer says Matt bribed witnesses in multiple federal court cases. When Matt appears to have lost everything, the King Pin blows up the hero's apartment, destroying all his possessions. Meanwhile, while Matt is fighting legal battles to save his reputation by day, Daredevil is combing the city to find the individual responsible for ruining his life by night.

Matt is unsure who he can and cannot trust, and eventually ends up in a dilapidated motel room with no heat in the dead of winter. He has only two dollars to his name. After discovering the King Pin is responsible for his downfall, Matt visits Wilson Fisk in his skyscraper. He intends to kill the villain, but Matt is sick, broken, and depressed, so King Pin nearly kills Matt. After the encounter, Matt, the once-powerful New York attorney and superhero crime fighter, is made homeless and sleeping on the streets.

Matt has broken ribs and is bleeding internally, yet he tells himself to keep moving and never give up. Eventually, he finds himself in a homeless mission within an inch of his life. His heart stops beating, but with the prayer of a nun, Matt returns to life. Over the weeks, Matt makes a slow recovery. He heals in a church basement in Hell's Kitchen. No one knows where Matt has gone and, for the most part, it seems no one cares.

Matt's body heals and he begins once again to build muscle. He's unable to practice law and has no access to his funds, so Matt remains in the shelter of the church and serves meals to the homeless. Overtime, Matt regains the persona of Daredevil. He does not get back the life he lived previously, but he does expose King Pin's plan to have him killed. Eventually, Matt wins, not because the villain was brought to justice, but because through it all, Matt survived. He may have cracked, but he never broke, and he continues to heal and grow.

Daredevil: Born Again does not have a fairytale ending. Instead, the ending is reflective of a survivor's journey of healing. Wilson Fisk retains power and money, but remains angry that he did not break his opponent in the way he believed he could. This corresponds to how perpetrators may not be brought to justice for their crimes but do become frustrated when their victim heals and thrives rather than remaining broken. Matt does not return to the high-rise apartment where he lived a dual life as a civil servant and a vigilante. Instead, he remains in Hell's Kitchen with Karen Page to help her battle her drug addiction. Like survivors, he does not return to his previous way of moving through the world, but instead, lives a life that is filled with more genuine joy.

Matt Murdock embodies what it means to transform and become the Master of Two Worlds. He embodies "The Man Without Fear," not because he is a blind man who fights injustice as the superhero, Daredevil, but because everything that previously defined who he was as an individual was stripped away, and still he did not lose sight of who he was and what he stood for. As a survivor seeking to heal, the goal is to achieve this level of transformation. In the healing process, this step is formally labeled **Resolution and Moving On**, but it is more than that. It means achieving **post-traumatic growth**.

Post-Traumatic Growth

Rather than post-traumatic stress, which is what occurs when an individual suffers a traumatic event, post-traumatic growth is the positive psychological change that can occur after an individual experiences a traumatic event. This does not mean a survivor should stop acknowledging that something traumatic and painful occurred in their life, or that they should live in a state of euphoric bliss, believing "everything happens for a reason" or that it's all part of "God's plan."

Psychologists Richard Tedeschi and Lawrence Calhoun discovered the phenomenon of post-traumatic growth and identified five categories of behaviors exhibited by those with this alternate view on life and growth:

1. **Survivors embrace new opportunities.** This does not mean the survivor has no fear or apprehension about new opportunities. Rather, they have the courage to face their fears rather than live in a constant state of fear.

2. **Survivors foster and nurture the growth of relationships.** They do not push away those they love and care for. They nurture the relationships they deem to be the most important. These relationships can be with friends, family, or loved ones.

3. **The knowledge that they have overcome hardship creates inner strength to continue to persevere.** This does not mean that the survivor views themselves as better and stronger than those around them. Instead, the survivor views their past as a testament that they may crack, but they will never be broken. This knowledge fuels them to continue to grow. Some individuals label this as **grit**.

4. **They gain a deeper appreciation for life.** This does not mean that each day of the survivor's life is perfect or they do not suffer bouts of depression and/or anxiety. It means the survivor knows that life will have good moments and bad. They appreciate life and see the benefit in both the good and bad. The survivor knows life is not, and cannot be, perfect. This allows them to appreciate what they have while simultaneously striving to achieve growth.

5. **Their relationship to religion and spirituality changes and evolves.** It is important to understand that there is a difference between religion and spirituality. Religion is usually attached to a doctrine or deity, while spirituality can be a connection to anything larger than one-

self. This means that a survivor can develop a larger connection to understanding their place in the cosmos, rather than developing a deeper connection to a specific religion such as Judaism, Islam, or Christianity.

There are two characters who offer examples of becoming the master of two worlds. Together, they show that this position does not guarantee post-traumatic growth. These characters are the villain Dr. Doom, and the Sorcerer Supreme, Dr. Stephen Strange.

CHAPTER SIXTEEN

Victor von Doom and Healing Childhood Wounds

In the book, *All About Love,* Bell Hooks discusses childhood trauma, love, and its long-term impact on males when she states,

> Many men in our culture never recover from childhood unkindness...From the moment little boys are taught they should not cry or express hurt, feelings of loneliness, or pain, that they must be tough, they are learning how to mask true feelings. Estrangement from feelings makes it easier for men to lie because they are often in a trance state, utilizing survival strategies of asserting manhood that they learned as boys...inwardly many men see themselves as victims of lovelessness...To embrace patriarchy, they must actively surrender the longing to love. [80]

---

80. Hooks, *All About Love.*

There is no character who exemplifies this statement more than Victor von Doom, the villain known as Dr. Doom who has permanently hidden his face behind the mask of a steel plate. His traumatic past can offer survivors an understanding of how an individual can become a master of two worlds, and still not have completed, or even begun, the difficult task of healing. Not all survivors follow the same steps of healing in the same order.

Victor von Doom is literally the master of two worlds: science and sorcery. As an adolescent and young adult, he learned to master both. However, it is important to note that Doom did not originate from wealth, but from extreme poverty and trauma. The comic series *The Book of Doom* retells the origins of the villain and the impact childhood trauma had on the trajectory of his entire existence.

Victor's mother, a traveling, persecuted gypsy of the country Latveria, learned sorcery, witchcraft, and black magic to help her fight the oppressive government that was abusing her people. She makes a deal with the demon Mephisto, who agrees to provide her with the ability to kill soldiers in a nearby village. But her abilities extend out of her control and kill all the children in the village as well. Wracked with guilt and unwilling to protect herself, she is stabbed to death. Mephisto sends her soul to hell for eternity. Victor's father, on the other hand, did not delve into the dark arts. Instead, he was a healer and leader of his people. When he failed to save the life of the Baron of Latveria's wife, he too was killed, leaving Victor orphaned very early in his life.

Victor locked away his anger and loneliness in much the same way that male survivors lock away their emotions because they are too painful to bear or because they believe emotions make them weak. Rather than heal from his childhood trauma, Victor learned to cope in the same manner as many survivors: through workaholism and perfectionism.

Victor became obsessed with unlocking the secrets of sorcery and the mysteries of science to save his mother's soul from the torments of hell. Although he is intelligent beyond belief, Victor pushes away all those who could help him achieve his goal. While in college, he amassed knowledge but refused to establish friendships and personal connections. Alone in his laboratory, Victor built a machine he believed would allow him to journey to the underworld. Since no one checked over his work, the device failed, exploded, and destroyed his dormitory, leaving his face permanently scarred into the mark of the demon, Mephisto.

Victor was dejected and believed himself to be a failure. He left America for Europe, hoping there he'd develop a new plan to save his mother. However, Victor never healed so the impact and scars of his childhood trauma only deepened, causing the wounds to become ever-more infected. Rather than nurture a relationship that would allow him to heal, Victor pushed away Valeria, his childhood love, and fell deeper within himself. He left the bandages on his face, remained constantly plagued by nightmares of his mother's torture, and searched desperately to acquire more knowledge.

Eventually, Victor ventured to Tibet where he became the master of a group of monks who spend their lives learning to integrate science with sorcery, rather than mastering healing of the inner self. Here, Victor von Doom becomes the villain Dr. Doom. He creates armor that shields the entirety of his body and assumes the metal mask that will never leave his face. It reveals only the scarred flesh around his eyes.

Although Doom uses his abilities to free Latveria from dictatorship, he still measures success by his failures. No matter how hard he tries, he is unable to free his mother's soul on his own. Although he has become the master of two worlds, he does not begin the process of healing from his childhood trauma until he asks for and accepts the help of an enemy-turned-ally, Dr. Stephen Strange.

Dr. Stephen Strange and the Journey of Healing

In *Strange Tales #115*, Stan Lee and Steve Ditko present readers with the origin of Dr. Stephen Strange, a fantastic American surgeon who has the ability to heal others through surgery but often refuses if his fees cannot be paid. Although talented, his arrogance overshadow his abilities.

Then, Strange damages the nerves of his hands in a car accident and is no longer able to perform surgery. He loses his capacity to find meaning in his life. His arrogance prevents him from becoming a consultant or teaching others. He states, "Stephen Strange assists nobody! I must be the best. The greatest! Or else nothing! I'll never consent to work for anyone else." [81]

Rather than learn to become the master of two worlds, Strange travels the world searching for a way to heal his hands and allow him to return to the life he once knew. No one can fix him until he hears of the Ancient One, an individual who can heal any ailment. Even the Ancient One is unable to heal the doctor's damaged hands, but the Ancient One offers to teach Strange how to become a master of the mystic arts. Strange refuses but is unable to return home due to an unexpected snowstorm.

---

81. Lee, Ditko, *Strange Tales #115*.

While in the temple of the Ancient One, Dr. Strange undergoes two transformations. One is physical and the other is psychological. First, the physical transformation occurs. Strange does not restore the use of his hands for surgery, but he learns the secrets of the mystic arts. His second transformation occurs when Strange learns to care for someone other than himself. After viewing the Ancient One's apprentice attempting to kill his master, Strange agrees to learn the mystic arts to save the Ancient One's life. This is how Dr. Strange become a sorcerer. He did not do it for himself, but to save the life of someone he barely knew, thereby ensuring humanity would not have to suffer the results of the Ancient One's murder.

Not only does Dr. Strange become the master of two worlds—Western medicine and the mystic arts—but he also experiences post-traumatic growth when he decides to become the master of his own healing. He makes the decision to put the needs of someone else before his own. This is what it means to become a survivor, heal from past traumatic experiences, and seek growth rather than perfection. Although the 1963 comic makes this process appear achievable in a week or a month, this form of monumental transformation occurs gradually over several years and numerous trials. This form of transformation requires self-reflection and self-love.

Many individuals have come to regard self-love as another form of selfishness. However, this is not the outcome when survivors venture along their journey of healing. When an individual learns to have empathy for others and love for themselves, that inner love reflects outward to nurture others. Bell Hooks explores the survivors' need for self-love in order to grow and heal when she states, "If one's goal is self-recovery, to be well in one's soul, honesty and realistically confronting lovelessness is part of the healing process." [82] Dr. Strange exemplifies this statement when he seeks to recover from the dysfunction of his hands, but is only able to truly heal when he addresses his lack of empathy for others, his own humility, and his need to learn to love himself and forgive his past mistakes.

The different journeys of Dr. Strange and Dr. Doom help to exemplify how becoming the master of two worlds does not equate to healing. Instead, healing requires an internal transformation that results in a form of post-traumatic growth. Survivors, in the same manner as Dr. Strange and Dr. Doom, learn to cope with the impact of their childhood sexual abuse when they procure and develop new talents to survive. Unlike fictional comic book characters, survivors do not learn to master the use of sorcery or the intricacies of thermal nuclear dynamics. Instead, they learn to remain sane and function in society without having to suppress their emotions and hide their identity behind a façade. Dr. Strange and Dr. Doom put aside their differences and worked together, which shows survivors what they need to do to reach the final level of growth on their journey of healing.

Dr. Strange, Dr. Doom, and Achieving Post-Traumatic Growth

In *Dr. Strange and Dr. Doom: Torment and Turmoil*, Dr. Strange and Dr. Doom work together to free from hell the soul of Victor von Doom's mother. The comic begins with the unlikely duo competing with other masters of the mystic arts to become the Sorcerer Supreme. This title identifies its bearer as

---

82. Hooks,

the most knowledgeable and skillful sorcerer on Earth. Dr. Strange is successful at accomplishing the task of becoming Sorcerer Supreme, while Dr. Doom comes in second. According to the rules of the tournament, Strange is required to fulfill any wish requested by Dr. Doom. Rather than ask for world domination or the destruction of Reed Richards and the Fantastic Four, Doom asks Dr. Strange to help him save his mother's soul. Surprised at the humble request, Dr. Strange agrees, and the two journey into the underworld.

While in hell, both Strange and Doom are forced to confront the demons of their past. Dr. Strange is forced to relive his selfish past. In the hellish version of his past, when he arrives to learn from the Ancient One, the master of mystic arts has already been murdered and Strange is thrown from the temple and not allowed to become a sorcerer. Dr. Doom is forced to decide whether he will betray Dr. Strange rather than free Doom's mother from an eternity of torture.

Dr. Strange succeeds at overcoming Mephisto's lies when he realizes that the light of truth, love, and humility are within him, not in his tools nor abilities to perform magic. With this realization, golden light shoots from his chest, destroying Mephisto's illusion and breaking his spell. Dr. Doom succeeds by relying on others and trusting them to make the right choice. Although Dr. Doom did betray Dr. Strange when he agreed to Mephisto's bargain, his mother would not allow her son to make the same mistake she had made. Once free, she refused to leave hell, redeeming her soul, and allowing her to atone for her past. Doom also secretly provided Dr. Strange with a device to free him from Mephisto's clutches.

Using *Torment and Turmoil* to explore post-traumatic growth shows how true healing only occurs when an individual learns the skills needed to love themselves and trust in others, two things survivors struggle to accept following their childhood trauma. Survivors must learn, in the same manner as Dr. Strange, that we do not need materialistic possessions to love ourselves. This journey of self-love and transformation is the key to recovery. This journey of healing can only be accomplished when survivors learn to love all parts of themselves. This is true love. This is true transformation. This is true recovery and healing. This is true post-traumatic growth.

This journey of healing and transformation is true not only for heroes such as Dr. Stephen Strange, but for those who are viewed by others and themselves as being a villain. Victor von Doom exemplifies this twice. First, against his better judgement and what he taught himself as a boy, he asks for help from Dr. Strange. Then, he trusts his mother to make the selfless decision to save his soul rather than her own. He achieves growth in the same manner as Dr. Strange because he learns that true healing cannot be achieved alone. Victor von Doom is arguably one of the smartest characters in the Marvel universe, but without humility and self-love, his healing could not be achieved. It would have been an impossibility. Failing to find self-love is the equivalent of survivors walling themselves off from the rest of the world and living behind a mask.

The parallel journies of Dr. Strange and Dr. Doom help to illustrate that no two survivors have the same path of healing. While Dr. Doom mastered the worlds of science and sorcery, his journey as a survivor rather than a villain was just the beginning. Dr. Strange, on the one hand, was well along his journey of healing, but the primary step of helping others was missing. Both characters illustrate that the goal of this journey is growth rather than a particular destination.

The journey you are on as a survivor is to be commendable because it will last a lifetime. The person you were will always be evolving. Examine your writing from the beginning of the guide and see how you have changed.

Writing Exercise #8: Revisiting Your Hero Code

In Part One: THE CALL TO HEALING you were asked to examine and write your hero code. Now that you are at the end of the guide, revisit your code. Rewrite your code to reflect your new outlook on healing, growth, and being a good man. Below is my revised code. It reflects how I see the world now that I have begun the difficult process of healing.

My Hero Code Now (Autobiographical)

Everyone is responsible for his or her own actions. It is my job to be the best version of myself I can be. This means doing what I *want* to do, not what I *have* to do. This does not mean being perfect or shirking my responsibilities, but it does mean knowing I have limits and self-worth. Realizing I have limitations does not make me weak. In fact, it makes me better, because it reminds me that I was unable to stop my abuse as a child and that I am strong now. Knowing, acknowledging, and accepting that I was sexually abused as a child does not mean blaming others for my abuse, but holding people accountable for their actions. I am a good person. And no matter what others may say (including my inner voice), it was not my fault. Men can be raped.

I have learned throughout this process to not be so hard on

myself; that having emotions and leaning on others for support is not a sign of weakness; and that loving someone does not mean absolving them from accountability for their actions. In the beginning I truly struggled with not only knowing but accepting that the abuse was not my fault. Now, I know it through and through. I am not only a survivor, but an overcomer who helps others realize their own inner superhero.

With Great Power...

At the end of the journey of healing from childhood sexual abuse it is said that survivors will be capable of resolving their past and moving on. While this is true, the sexual abuse endured by survivors will remain a part of who they are. It will shape their actions, reactions, and views. While the abuse was a tragedy no child should have to endure, it gives survivors an opportunity to provide perspectives that others, who have not experienced and healed from sexual trauma, cannot possess. Being a male survivor of child sexual abuse means you are stronger because you survived and made the choice to heal from your past trauma rather than perpetuate the cycle. This makes you a good man. I would like to end this guide with my favorite poem and a reminder of what it means to be a good man.

"If–"
By Rudyard Kipling

If you can keep your head when all about you
Are losing theirs and blaming it on you,

If you can trust yourself when all men doubt you,
But make allowance for their doubting too;
If you can wait and not be tired by waiting,
Or being lied about, don't deal in lies,
Or being hated, don't give way to hating,
And yet don't look too good, nor talk too wise:

If you can dream and not make dreams your master;
If you can think—and not make thoughts your aim;
If you can meet with Triumph and Disaster
And treat those two imposters just the same;
If you can bear to hear the truth you've spoken
Twisted by knaves to make a trap for fools,
Or watch the things you give life to, broken,
And stoop and build'em with worn-out tools:

If you can make one heap of all your winnings
And risk it on a turn of pitch-and-toss,
And lose, and start again at your beginnings
And never breathe a word about your loss;
If you can force your heart and nerve and sinew
To serve your turn long after they are gone,
And so hold on when there is nothing in you
Except the will which says to them: 'Hold on!'

If you can talk with crowds and keep your virtue,
Or walk with Kings—nor lose the common touch,
If neither foes nor loving friends can hurt you,
If all men count with you, but none too much;
If you can fill the unforgiving minute
With sixty seconds' worth of distance run
Yours is the Earth and everything that's in it,

And —which is more— you'll be a Man, my son!

Further reading

The comics and books referenced throughout this guide are listed below. As I mentioned previously, I am not a psychiatrist, therapist, psychologist, or counselor. I am not even an expert in all things and characters that exist in the Marvel universe. I am simply a male survivor attempting to make a positive difference in the lives of others. This guide was written to help male survivors, like myself, understand the trauma of their sexual abuse in a manner they find familiar, comfortable, fun, and beneficial along their path of recovery. Use this list of sources to buy, read, and give respect to the artists and writers who created the fantastically detailed Marvel universe. Use this list to further your reading of comics and to acquire more tools to accompany you along your journey of healing.

Sources

Allen Nancy et al. *Spider-Man and Power Pack*. Marvel, 1984.

American Foundation for Suicide Prevention. "Suicide and Statistics," afsp.org/suicide-statistics. Accessed February 14, 2023.

Bass, Ellen, and Laura Davis. *The Courage to Heal: A Guide for Women Survivors of Child Sexual Abuse*. William Morrow, 1994.

Ben-Shahar, Tal. *Happier: Learn the Secrets to Daily Joy and Lasting Fulfillment*. McGraw Hill, 2007.

Brubaker, Ed, and Pablo Raimondi. *Books of Doom #1-6*. Marvel, 2005-2006.

Campbell, Joseph. *The Hero with A Thousand Faces*. Pantheon Books, 1949.

DeFalco, Tom, and Ron Frenz. "All My Past Remembered." *The Amazing Spider-Man #259*. Marvel, 1984.

DeMatteis, J.M., and Mike Zeck. "Part Five: Thunder." *The Amazing Spider-Man #294*. Marvel, 1987.

—. "Part Four: Resurrection." *Web of Spider-Man #32*. Marvel, 1987.

—. "Part One: The Coffin." *Web of Spider-Man #31*. Marvel, 1987.

—. "Part Six: Ascending." *Peter Parker the Spectacular Spider Man #132*. Marvel, 1987.

—. "Part Three: Descent." *Peter Parker the Spectacular Spider Man #131*. Marvel, 1987.

—. "Part Two: Crawling." *The Amazing Spider-Man #293*. Marvel, 1987.

DeMatteis, J.M., and Sal Buscema. "The Child Within: Parts 1-6." *The Spectacular Spider-Man #178-184*. Marvel, 1991-1992.

Herman, Judith. *Trauma and Recovery*. Basic Books, 1992.

Hooks, Bell. *All About Love*. William Morrow, 2018.

James, Gerod, et al. *Marvel Comics Presents: Weapon X #76-84*. Marvel, 1991

Jenkins, Paul, and Andy Kubert. "The Inner Child." *Origins #2*. Marvel, 2001.

Jenkins, Paul, and John Watson. *Civil War: Front Line #1*. Marvel, 2006.

—. *Civil War: Front Line #2*. Marvel, 2006.

Jenking, Paul, et al. "The Hill". *Wolverine: The Origin #1*.

Marvel, 2001.

—. "Inner Child". *Wolverine: The Origin #2*. Marvel 2001.

Kimmel, Michael. "Raise Your Son to be a Good Man, not a 'Real Man.'" New York Magazine, 2018. www.thecut.com/2018/03/teaching-our-sons-to-be-good-men.html

Kipling, Rudyard. "If." Doubleday, Page & Company, 1910.

Layton, Bob et al. "Demon in a Bottle." *Iron Man #128*. Marvel, 1979.

Lee, Stan, and Bill Everett. "The Origin of Daredevil." *Daredevil #1*. Marvel, 1964.

Lee, Stan, and Gene Colan. "The Origin of the Silver Surfer." *Silver Surfer #1*. Marvel, 1987.

Lee, Stan, and Jack Kirby. "The Coming of Galactus." *The Fantastic Four #48*. Marvel, 1966.

—. "The Hulk." *The Incredible Hulk #1*. Marvel, 1962.

—. "Who is the Real Don Blake." *Thor#159*. Marvel, 1966.

Lee, Stan, and John Romita Sr. "Unmasked at Last." *The Amazing Spider-Man #87*. Marvel, 1970

Lee, Stan, and Steve Ditko. *Amazing Fantasy #15*. Marvel, 1977.

—. *Journey into Mystery #124*. Marvel, 1966.

—. "Kraven the Hunter." *The Amazing Spider-Man #15*. Marvel, 1964.

—. "The Coming of the Scorpion!" *The Amazing Spider-Man*

#20. Marvel, 1963.

—. "The Spider-Man Goes Mad." *The Amazing Spider-Man* #24. Marvel, 1965.

Lee, Stan, et al. "The Spider and the Burglar." *The Amazing Spider-Man* #200. Marvel, 1980.

Lee, Stan, et al. *Strange Tales #115*. Marvel, 1963.

Lieber, Larry, et al. *Journey into Mystery #90*. Marvel, 1963.

Lieber, Larry, et al. *Tales of Suspense #39*. Marvel, 1959.

Lieber, Larry, et al. *Journey Into Mystery #83*. Marvel, 1962.

Loeb, Jeph, and Tim Sale. *Captain America: White*. Marvel, 2008.

—. *Daredevil: Yellow*. Marvel, 2002.

—. *Hulk: Gray*. Marvel, 2004.

—. Marvel, 2003.

Mantlo, Bill, and Mike Mignola. "Monster." *The Incredible Hulk #312*. Marvel, 1985.

Mantlo, Bill, and Sal Buscema. "And Here There Be Demons." *The Incredible Hulk #308*. Marvel, 1985.

Miller, Frank, and David Mazzucchelli. "Born Again." *Daredevil #227-231*. Marvel, 1986.

Pollack, William. *Real Boys: Rescuing Our Sons from the Myths of Boyhood*. Owl Books, 1999.

Porges, Stephen. *The Pocket Guide to the Polyvagal Theory:*

The Transformative Power of Feeling Safe. W.W. Norton & Company, 2017.

Rogers Jr., Kenneth. *How to Kill Your Batman: A Guide for Male Survivors of Childhood Sexual Abuse Using Batman to Heal Hypervigilance*. Strategic Book Publishing, 2019.

—. *Raped Black Male: A Memoir*. Strategic Book Publishing, 2016.

—. *Thoughts in Italics*, Publish America, 2007.

Rosenberg, Robin, et al.. *What is a Superhero?* Oxford University Press, 2013.

Schwartz, Arielle. *The Complex PTSD Workbook*. Althea, 2017.

Stern, Roger, et al. *Dr. Strange and Dr. Doom*: Triumph and Torment. Marvel, 1989.

Treleaven, David. *Trauma-Sensitive Mindfulness: Practices for Safe and Transformative Healing*. W.W. Norton & Company, 2018.

Kolk, Bessel van der. *The Body Keeps the Score: Brain, Mind, and Body in the Healing of Trauma*. Penguin, 2014.

Williams, Mary Beth, and Soili Poijula. *The PTSD Workbook: Simple Effective Techniques for Overcoming Traumatic Stress Symptoms*. New Harbinger, 2016.

Effective Techniques for Overcoming Traumatic Stress Symptoms. New Harbinger, 2016.

Glossary

The Marvel universe is vast in size and characters. This glossary is meant to help reduce obstacles for readers who want to use this guide but are unfamiliar with the nuances of Marvel's characters and their abilities. If there are any inaccuracies here or throughout this guide, I am sorry. The mistakes were not made intentionally. I continue to grow and learn along this worthwhile journey.

A

Abyss: stage in the hero and survivor's journey in which the individual experiences uncertainty, uneasiness, and sadness.

Alexander van Tilberg: character of the Marvel universe. He is the former husband of Bethany Cabe. He was the West German Junior Ambassador to the U.S., and was addicted to alcohol. He died following a fatal car crash.

Alicia Masters: character of the Marvel universe. She is the blind girlfriend/wife of Fantastic Four member Benjamin Grimm.

All-or-Nothing Thinking: cognitive distortion that occurs when a survivor thinks of events in absolute, black-and-white terms.

Ancient One: character of the Marvel universe. He trains Dr. Stephen Strange in the mystic arts.

Apotheosis: stage in the hero and survivor's journey when the individual is filled with joy after accomplishing a difficult task.

Arrival Fallacy: theory proposed by Tal Ben-Shahar in his book *Happier* that explains how individuals can live under the false belief that reaching a valued destination can sustain happiness.

Asgard: fictional location in the Marvel universe that is home to Norse gods, including Thor, Loki, and Odin.

Association: the reintegration of traumatic thoughts into a survivor's memories.

B

Benjamin Grimm: superhero of the Marvel universe. He is known as the Thing. He is a member of the Fantastic Four.

Ben Parker: character of the Marvel universe. He is known as Uncle Ben and is Peter Parker's uncle.

Bethany Cabe: character of the Marvel universe. She is the former girlfriend of Tony Stark. She helps him conquer his alcohol addiction.

Betty Ross: character of the Marvel universe. She is the daughter of General "Thunderbolt" Ross and girlfriend/wife of Bruce Banner.

Blame: cognitive distortion in which the survivor places the fault of their actions on others while denying their role in the problem.

Brian Banner: character of the Marvel universe. He is the abusive father of Bruce Banner.

Bruce Banner: superhero of the Marvel universe. He was bombarded with gamma radiation and can now transform into the Hulk.

Bucky: hero of the Marvel universe. He was the teenage sidekick to Captain America

C

Captain America: superhero of the Marvel universe. He is often referred to as the First Avenger. He received Super Soldier serum in 1943 as private Steve Rogers and became a U.S. Army soldier with heightened abilities.

Charles Xavier: superhero of the Marvel universe. He is the founder of the superhero team known as the X-Men.

Child, Parent, Adult (CPA) Thoughts: different ways that survivors think and reason.

Cognitive Behavior Therapy (CPT): form of therapy that recognizes the connection between an individual's thoughts, behaviors, and how they feel.

Cognitive Distortions: mental filters that increase misery, anxiety, and/or depression.

D

Daredevil: superhero of the Marvel universe. He uses his heightened senses and agility to fight crime; he is sometimes referred to as the Man Without Fear.

Decision to Heal: stage of the healing process in which the survivor makes the conscious choice to begin the journey of healing.

Dissociation: the separation of a survivor from their traumatic memories, thoughts, and emotions.

Dissociative Identity Disorder (DID): mental disability in which a survivor creates different personalities to cope with the pain of their trauma.

Doctor Curt Connors: character of the Marvel universe. He transforms into the villain the Lizard.

Doctor Doom: villain of the Marvel universe. He is an enemy of the Fantastic Four. He has mastered advanced sciences and the mystic arts.

Doctor Otto Octavius: villain of the Marvel universe. He is known as Doc Ock.

Doctor Farley Stillwell: character of the Marvel universe. He is hired by James Jonah Jameson to doctor the villain, the Scorpion.

Donald Blake: character of the Marvel universe. He is the alter ego of the Norse god Thor.

Doublethink/Double Self: theory created by Judith Herman, PhD, in which a survivor develops the ability to create and keep positive thoughts and memories alongside those of utter despair to preserve the possibility of hope.

Dr. Abraham Cornelius: character of the Marvel universe. He is a senior scientist for the Weapon X program.

Dr. Ashley Kafka: character of the Marvel universe. She helps heal Edward Whelan of his alter ego Vermin. She also councils Peter Parker back to sanity after he was drugged by the Green Goblin.

Dr. Leonard Samson: character of the Marvel universe. He is a skilled psychiatrist.

Dr. Ludwig Rinehart: character of the Marvel universe. He is a fictional doctor created by the villain Mysterio.

Dr. Stephen Strange: superhero of the Marvel universe. He is a master of the dark arts and is the Sorcerer Supreme.

E

Edward Whelan: character of the Marvel universe. He is sexually abused as a child and transforms into the villain Vermin as an adult after being experimented on by the villain Zemo.

Elizabeth Howlett: character of the Marvel universe. She is the mother of James Howlett (Wolverine).

Emergency Stage: stage of the healing process in which the survivor experiences extreme uncontrolled feelings of loneliness, sadness, depression, or anxiety that cannot be explained.

Exiles: part of internal family system therapy in which a portion of the personality is labeled all things they believe to be bad.

F

Façade: the persona a survivor uses to hide their identity.

Fight, Flight, Freeze: possible reactions to an individual's exposure to danger in which they either fight for safety, run away, or remain frozen.

Firefighters: part of internal system therapy in which a portion of an individual's personality is assigned to suppress the negative emotions and thoughts of the exile.

Foggy Nelson: character of the Marvel universe. He is the best friend and law partner of Matthew Murdock (Daredevil).

Fortune-Telling: cognitive distortion in which the survivor arbitrarily attempts to predict the future and often assumes the worse.

G

Galactus: villain of the Marvel universe. He devours entire planets and its inhabitants for his sustenance.

Gayle Watson: character of the Marvel universe. She is the sister of Mary Jane Watson.

General "Thunderbolt" Ross: character of the Marvel universe. He is the father of Betty Ross and a general in the United States Army.

Glow: character of the Marvel universe that is a member of the Triad. Glow exists in Bruce Banner's consciousness and provides him with a sense of safety.

Goblin: character in the Marvel universe who is a member of the Triad. Goblin exists in Bruce Banner's consciousness and attempts to protect him from the abuse of his father through fear, which inspires Bruce to fight for survival.

Green Goblin: villain of the Marvel universe. He hates Spider-Man and was first embodied by Norman Osbourn, and later, by his son Harry Osbourn.

Guardian: character of the Marvel universe that is a member of the Triad. Guardian exists in Bruce Banner's consciousness in an attempt to protect him from the abuse of his father through the use of rational thought to ensure preservation.

Gwen Stacey: character of the Marvel universe. She was the girlfriend of Peter Parker. She was killed by the Green Goblin.

H

Harry Osbourn: character of the Marvel universe. He is the son of Norman Osbourn and eventually becomes the villain Green Goblin.

Hulk: superhero of the Marvel universe. He comes into being when Bruce Banner becomes angry.

Human Torch: superhero of the Marvel universe. He is a member of the Fantastic Four. He has the ability to ignite into a flame. His real name is Johnny Storm.

I

Internal Family System (IFS) Therapy: system of therapy that works to unite a survivor's firefighter, manager, and exile into one complete Self.

Invisible Woman: superhero of the Marvel universe. She is a member of the Fantastic Four.

Iron Man: superhero of the Marvel universe. He is the billionaire-playboy Tony Stark in a superpowered, technologically advanced suit of armor.

J

James Buchanan Barnes: character of the Marvel universe. He is the alter ego of Captain America's sidekick, Bucky.

James Howlett: character of the Marvel universe. He grows up to become the superhero Wolverine.

James Jonah Jameson: character of the Marvel universe. He owns *The Daily Bugle* and hates Spider-Man.

Jane Foster: character of the Marvel universe. She is the love interest of the Norse god Thor.

Jarvis: character of the Marvel universe. He is the personal butler of Tony Stark.

Johnny Storm: character of the Marvel universe. He is the alter ego of the superhero the Human Torch.

Judge: villain of the Marvel universe. He is the father and sexual abuser of Edward Whelan.

K

Karen Page: character of the Marvel universe. She is Matt Murdoch's love interest and secretary.

King Pin: villain of the Marvel universe. He is the crime boss of New York City and operates under the guise of businessman Wilson Fisk.

Kraven the Hunter: villain of the Marvel universe. He hates Spider-Man and prides himself on being the world's greatest hunter. His real name is Sergei Kravinoff.

L

Lizard: villain of the Marvel universe. He was created when Dr. Curt Conners crossed his DNA with that of a lizard to develop cellular regeneration.

Logan: character of the Marvel universe. He is believed to be the father of Wolverine. Logan is also the name often given to Wolverine despite his real name being James Howlett.

M

Mac Gargan: character of the Marvel universe. He transforms into the villain Scorpion following experimentation by Dr. Farley Stillwell.

Madeline Watson: character of the Marvel universe. She is the mother of Mary Jane Watson.

Managers: part of internal family system therapy in which a portion of the individual's personality is assigned to maintain order and productivity throughout the survivor's life.

May Parker: character of the Marvel universe. She is known as Aunt May, and is Peter Parker's aunt.

Matt Murdock: character of the Marvel universe. He is a blind lawyer from Hell's Kitchen, New York. Matt is the alter ego of the superhero Daredevil.

Mary Jane Watson: character of the Marvel universe. She is the girlfriend/wife of Peter Parker.

Mephisto: villain of the Marvel universe. He presides over hell.

Mind Reading: cognitive disorder in which the survivor attempts to predict the actions of others to feel more in control of his life.

Miss Hines: character of the Marvel universe. She is one of the lead researchers of the Weapon X project.

Mjolnir: the magical hammer of the Norse god, Thor.

Mr. Fantastic: superhero of the Marvel universe. He is the leading member of the Fantastic Four, has the ability of elasticity, and is scientist Reed Richards.

Mysterio: villain of the Marvel universe. He creates illusions to kill the superhero Spider-Man.

N

Norman Osbourn: character of the Marvel universe. He becomes the villain Green Goblin.

Norrin Radd: character of the Marvel universe. He becomes the superhero Silver Surfer when he attempts to save his planet from the destruction of Galactus.

Nurse Meachum: villain of the Marvel universe. She was Bruce Banner's abusive nurse.

O

Odin: character of the Marvel universe. He is the Norse god who rules Asgard. Odin is Thor's father.

P

Personalization: cognitive distortion in which the survivor blames himself for things he was not entirely responsible for.

Peter Parker: character of the Marvel universe. He becomes the superhero Spider-Man after being bit by a radioactive spider.

Post-Traumatic Growth: the positive psychological change that can occur after an individual experiences a traumatic event.

Post-Traumatic Stress Disorder: negative psychological change that occurs after an individual experiences a traumatic event.

Professor: villain of the Marvel universe. He is the lead researcher in the Weapon X project.

Q

Quentin Beck: character of the Marvel universe. He becomes the villain Mysterio.

R

Rebecca Banner: character of the Marvel universe. She is the mother of Bruce Banner.

Red Skull: villain of the Marvel universe. He fought with the Nazis, against Captain America, during World War II.

Reed Richards: character of the Marvel universe. He becomes the leader of the superhero team Fantastic Four after traveling through a ban of radiation in space.

Rick Jones: character of the Marvel universe. He causes Bruce Banner to be bombarded with gamma radiation after Bruce travels onto a restricted-access bomb-testing site of the United States Army.

Road of Trials: step in a hero and survivor's journey of healing in which the individual takes risks, makes mistakes, and gains experience.

Rose O'Hara: character of the Marvel universe. She is the nurse and eventual love interest of James Howlett, the young boy who grows up to become the hero Wolverine.

S

Sandman: villain of the Marvel universe. He battles Spider-Man by transforming into sand.

Scorpion: villain of the Marvel universe. He battles Spider-Man as a giant scorpion. His real name is Mac Gargan.

Sergei Kravinoff: character of the Marvel universe. He battles Spider-Man as the villain Kraven the Hunter.

S.H.I.E.L.D.: fictional government agency in the Marvel universe that stands for Strategic Homeland Intervention, Enforcement, and Logistics Division.

Should/Shouldn't Have Statements: cognitive distortion in which the survivor uses "should," "ought to," "must," and "have to" statements to criticize himself and his actions.

Silver Surfer: superhero of the Marvel universe. He becomes endowed with the Power Cosmic by the villain Galactus after he (as Norrin Radd) attempts to save his planet from destruction.

Sorcerer Supreme: title given to the Marvel character who is deemed to be the master of the mystic arts.

Spider-Man: superhero of the Marvel universe. His secret identity is Peter Parker.

Steve Rogers: character of the Marvel universe. He becomes the hero Captain America when he takes Super Soldier serum.

Subjective Units of Distress Scale (SUDS): scale used to help survivors identify and understand their emotions.

Sue Richards: character of the Marvel universe. She becomes the superhero the Invisible Woman after traveling through a ban of radiation in space. She is a member of the Fantastic Four.

T

Thing: superhero of the Marvel universe. He is a member of the Fantastic Four and has thick skin in the form of bricks and super strength. His real name is Benjamin Grimm.

Tony Stark: character of the Marvel universe. He becomes the superhero Iron Man after escaping from a war prison during the Vietnam War.

Thor: superhero of the Marvel universe. He is a Norse god from the planet Asgard.

V

Vermin: villain of the Marvel universe. He resembles a giant rat and is the living embodiment of the repressed memories and emotions of Edward Whelan.

Victor von Doom: character of the Marvel universe. He is from the country of Latvaria and eventually becomes the villain Dr. Doom. He yearns to save his mother from villain Mephisto.

Vulture: villain of the Marvel universe. He flies with the use of a vulture suit and tries to kill Spider-Man.

W

Weapon X: character of the Marvel universe. This is the name James Howlett is given when he is made into a living weapon after being experimented on and brainwashed.

Wilson Fisk: villain of the Marvel universe. He uses his power as a businessman to become the King Pin of crime.

Wolverine: superhero of the Marvel universe. He is a mutant who can heal quickly. He has an adamantium skeleton and blades extending from his knuckles. He fights on the superhero team the X-Men.

X

X-Men: superhero team of the Marvel universe made up of mutants with special abilities.

Kenneth Rogers, Jr. is a father, husband, teacher, and survivor of childhood sexual abuse. Kenneth teaches English in Baltimore, MD, and holds a Master's in education from Johns Hopkins University. To date, Kenneth has written and published thirteen books, winning over twenty national indie book awards. His previous titles include the young adult trilogy Chronicles of the Last Liturian, the science fiction novel, Sequence, and the memoir, Raped Black Male.